THE NEW HISTORY OF
THE ITALIAN SOUTH
THE MEZZOGIORNO REVISITED

THE NEW HISTORY OF THE ITALIAN SOUTH
The Mezzogiorno Revisited

Edited by

Robert Lumley and
Jonathan Morris

UNIVERSITY
of
EXETER
PRESS

First published in 1997 by
University of Exeter Press
Reed Hall, Streatham Drive
Exeter EX4 4QR, Devon, UK

University of Exeter Press gratefully acknowledges support for this book
from the Italian Cultural Institute in London

British Library Cataloguing in Publication Data
A catalogue record of this book is available from the British Library

ISBN 0 85989 506 8

Typeset in 11 on 13 pt Plantin by Exe Valley Dataset Ltd, Exeter

Printed and bound in Great Britain by BPC Wheatons Ltd, Exeter

Contents

Illustrations

Preface

The New History of the Italian South: The Mezzogiorno Revisited owes its origins to a series of seminars organized by the editors at the Italian Cultural Institute in London. Papers from the seminars 'Liberal Italy and the *Mezzogiorno*' held in 1993 are joined by Paolo Macry's paper on Naples given to the second series entitled 'Historical Perspectives on the Italian City' of 1995. Due to the support of the Institute and its then director, Professor Francesco Villari, we were able to create a forum that brought scholars from Britain and Italy together in lively discussion. Looking back, there was the excitement of contact with some of the finest of a younger generation of historians and with work that was radically redefining the history of Southern Italy. In addition there was a keen sense of the political and cultural issues at stake and their implications for the role of the historian as public intellectual.

Since they were first prepared, the papers have been revised and elaborated for publication. Furthermore, we decided to ask Marta Petrusewicz if she would contribute a chapter to the collection, given the importance of the debate on the *latifondo* and of her part in it. Jonathan Morris's introductory essay was then designed to put the new historiography and its challenge to the stereotypes of *meridionalismo* into context.

Editing was made a pleasurable task by the authors, and we would like to thank them for their good humour and helpfulness. Francesco Villari was generous and enthusiastic in his support for the seminars and then for the idea of making them available in book form. University of Exeter Press, whom we approached with the help of Luisa Quartermaine, has patiently encouraged the project, thanks in particular to Simon Baker and Genevieve Davey. The copy editing by Jane Bainbridge greatly sharpened up the text. Lastly, we would like to acknowledge the assistance of the Department of History and the Department of Italian at University College, London, and to add that this story of departmental collaboration had a happy outcome, in that it led to the setting up of the inter-disciplinary Centre for Italian Studies at UCL. We look forward to this publication being a precedent for the future.

Gabriella Gribaudi's 'The *Mezzogiorno* as seen by Insiders and Outsiders' is translated by Allan Cameron with some revision and additional translation by Robert Lumley (a considerably abbreviated version entitled 'Images of the South' appeared in D. Forgacs and R. Lumley (eds.), *Italian Cultural Studies:An Introduction* (Oxford, 1996).

Robert Lumley and Jonathan Morris, 1997

Notes on Editors and Contributors

Fulvio Cammarano teaches Political History at the University of Bologna and is author of *Il progresso moderato. Un'opposizione liberale nella svolta dell'Italia crispina* (Bologna, 1990).

John Dickie teaches Italian Studies at University College, London, and his history of stereotypes of the South in Liberal Italy is due to be published by Italian Perspectives.

Gabriella Gribaudi teaches Modern and Contemporary History at the University of Naples and is author of *A Eboli. Il mondo meridionale in cent'anni di trasformazioni* (Venice, 1990). She is on the editorial board of *Meridiana*.

Robert Lumley teaches Italian Studies at University College, London, and is author of *States of Emergency. Cultures of Revolt in Italy, 1968–78* (London, 1990).

Paolo Macry teaches Modern History at the Federico II University of Naples and is author of *Ottocento. Famiglie, élite e patrimoni a Napoli* (Turin, 1988).

Jonathan Morris teaches Modern European History at University College, London, and is author of *The Political Economy of Shopkeeping in Milan, 1886–1922* (Cambridge, 1993).

Paolo Pezzino teaches Modern History at the University of Pisa and is the author of *Una certa reciprocità di favori. Mafia e modernizzazione nella Sicilia postunitaria* (Milan, 1990). He is on the editorial board of *Meridiana*.

Marta Petrusewicz teaches Modern History at Hunter College, City University of New York and is author of *Latifundium: Moral Economy and Material Life in a European Periphery* (Michigan, 1996).

Chronology of Events in Southern Italy, 1799–1915

1799	French occupation of the Kingdom of Naples and establishment of the Parthenopean Republic.
1799	Fall of the Republic and return of the Bourbons aided by the British navy.
1806	Napoleon reoccupies the Kingdom of Naples and makes his brother Joseph head of government.
1806, 2 August	Bonaparte's government abolishes feudalism in the Kingdom of Naples
1815, 2 June	Ferdinand IV of Bourbon enters Naples.
1816, 8 December	Birth of the Kingdom of the Two Sicilies
1816, 12 December	Establishment in the Kingdom of Naples of administrative system based on the French model.
1820, 15 July	Popular insurrection in Palermo against the central government.
1838, 7 May	Ferdinand II consolidates centralization of administration of Sicily
1848, 11 February	Ferdinand II concedes constitution.

1848, 13 April	Sicilian parliament declares island's independence.
1848, 16 April	Parliament and National Guard dissolved by the king in Naples.
1860, 4 April	Insurrection in Palermo suppressed but revolt spreads across Sicily.
1860, 11 May	Garibaldi's expedition disembarks at Marsala.
1860, 7 September	Garibaldi enters Naples.
1860, 21 October	Plebiscite followed by incorporation of the Kingdom of the Two Sicilies into the Kingdom of Italy.
1860, 26 October	Meeting of Garibaldi and Victor Emmanuel at Teano. Handover of power and disbanding of the Garibaldian troops.
1860, October	Abolition of tariffs protecting industry in the South.
1861, 17 January	Trade treaty with France favourable to Southern agriculture.
1861, 27 January	General election to elect first Italian Parliament based on suffrage of 8 per cent of male population. Decisive victory for the moderate Right.
1861–1866	Brigandage in the South, especially in Puglia, Molise, Basilicata and Campania. 116,000 troops used to put down insurgency.

1861–1877	Sale of hundreds of thousands of hectares of church lands.
1872	Publication of Pasquale Villari's 'La scuola e la questione sociale in Italia'.
1876, 25 March	Formation of the first government of the Left under Agostino Depretis after the defeat of the Right in Parliament.
1876, 5 November	General elections; victory of the parliamentary Left with 70 per cent of the vote.
1876	Publication of Pasquale Villari's *Le lettere meridionali*; Leopoldo Franchetti's and Sidney Sonnino's *La Sicilia nel 1876*; Cesare Lombroso's *Trattato antropologico sperimentale dell'uomo delinquente*.
1877	Publication of Jessie Mario-White's *La miseria di Napoli*.
1878, 9 January	Death of Victor Emmanuel II.
1881	Census shows illiteracy rates of 75 per cent in Campania, 80 per cent in Puglia, 85 per cent in Calabria (compared to 37 per cent in Lombardy).
1882, 22 January	Electoral reform lowers voting age to twenty-one, reduces the tax threshold and introduces educational qualification. Suffrage extended to 28 per cent of male population.
1883, 28 October	Inauguration of railway running from Rome to Campobasso.

1884	Cholera outbreak in Naples and death of 8,000 within three years.
1887, 26 January	Massacre of 500 Italian troops at Dogali in Eritrea.
1887, 21 June	Tariffs raised on grain, followed by new general tariff.
1887, 7 August	Francesco Crispi becomes prime minister.
1888, 18 February	Beginning of the trade war with France.
1888, December	Reform of local administration: widening of the suffrage and election of mayors for the first time.
1888, 30 December	Bill recognizing the freedom to emigrate.
1892, May	Spread of 'Fasci' (union organization of agricultural workers) in Sicily.
1892, 14 August	Foundation of the Italian Socialist Party in Genoa.
1893, 9–25 December	Repression of popular uprisings in Sicily, with state of siege and outlawing of Fasci declared by Crispi government in following January.
1894	The journal *Riforma sociale* founded by Francesco Saverio Nitti.
1896, 1 March	Defeat of Italian army with heavy losses by Abyssinians at Adowa.

1896, 5 March	Resignation of Crispi.
1898	Publication of Alfredo Niceforo's *Italia barbara contemporanea*.
1898, 26 April	Outbreak of popular protest and bread riots spread from Romagna to Puglia and Campania as well as to Lombardy and Piedmont. Repression and exceptional laws that remove civil rights.
1900	First issue of the review *Nord e Sud*.
1900, 31 January	New law to regulate emigration; data of the general census shows that over 2,251,000 had emigrated in previous decade, mainly from the South.
1901	Average illiteracy rates of 70 per cent in the South (compared to 40 per cent in the North) according to the general census.
1902, September	Visit to Basilicata by the prime minister, Guiseppe Zanardelli.
1903, 1 January	Gaetano Salvemini in *Critica sociale* champions universal suffrage in local government as weapon against the *camorra*.
1903, 3 November	Giovanni Giolitti becomes prime minister.
1904, 31 March	Special law for Naples and Basilicata: programme of public works, tax alleviation, and credit facilitation.

1906, 17 July	Special law for Calabria.
1906, 8 March	Government proposals for the South: easing of tax and credit burdens on smallholders.
1906	Opening of Bagnoli steel plant near Naples.
1908, 28 December	Earthquake kills 150,000 in Messina and Reggio Calabria.
1909, 14 March	Publication of *Il ministero della malavita*, Salvemini's polemic against the Giolitti government's use of political corruption in the South to buy votes.
1910, October	Following the national congress, Salvemini leaves the Italian Socialist Party over policies towards the South.
1913, 30 June	Electoral reform: vote extended to all males over thirty and to those over twenty-one on completion of military service or having the requisite educational qualifications.
1915, 24 May	Italy enters war against Austro-Hungarians.

Glossary

bracciante (pl. **braccianti**)   agricultural wage labourer
camorra   powerful Neapolitan *mafia*-type organization that had its origins during the Spanish occupation and became an established force in the eighteenth century
colono (pl. **coloni**)   small tenant farmer
comune (pl. *comuni*)   local council
Destra   the political Right who held power following Unification
Fasci   Agricultural worker associations formed in Sicily in 1892
gabellotto (pl. **gabellotti**)   middlemen who sublet land leased from the *latifondo* (q.v.)
intendente (pl. **intendenti**)   the administrative head of a province in some Italian states before Unification
italianità   'Italian-ness'
latifondismo   system of economic production and social relations based on the *latifondo* (q.v.)
latifondista (pl. **latifondisti**)   wealthy landowner, owner of a *latifondo* (q.v.)
latifondo (pl. **latifondi**)   a vast landed estate which usually combined cereal-growing and animal husbandry. The characteristic form of agricultural enterprise in Southern Italy
masseria (pl. **masserie**) a large farm complete with its own buildings
meridionalismo   an intellectual concept that explains the idiosyncrasies of Southern Italy in relation to the rest of the country
meridionalista (pl. **meridionalisti**) writer studying the specific social and economic problems of the Italian South
Meridione   Southern Italy
Mezzogiorno   Southern Italy
'ndrangheta   Calabrian *mafia*-type organization
questione meridionale   the Southern question
Risorgimento   period between the end of the eighteenth century 1870 leading to the Unification of Italy
scioltezza (adj. **sciolto**)   lack of social bonds, of attachments outside the family
sicilianità   'Sicilian-ness'
Sinistra   the political Left that came to power in 1876
Sud   the South
università   university in the medieval sense of the word, a corporation or an association of arts, trades, or crafts

1

Challenging *Meridionalismo*
Constructing a New History for Southern Italy

JONATHAN MORRIS

A significant shift in interpretations of the history of Southern Italy (known in Italian as the *Mezzogiorno*) took place in the past decade. This volume makes available in English a selection of essays by some of the scholars who contributed to this development. It is intended as a reader on the new historiography of the South, but it does not pretend to a comprehensiveness that, given the diversity of current approaches, would be merely illusory. Most of the analyses are concerned with the South's 'long nineteenth century' during which the abolition of feudalism under Napoleonic rule was followed by the reforms of the restored Bourbon state, the upheavals of the *Risorgimento*, and agrarian, political and demographic crises during the Liberal era. (An outline chronology of these events is provided at the beginning of the volume.) This essay will analyse the common features of the revisionist literature, and acts as an introduction to the pieces that follow.

The South became an object of special study soon after Giuseppe Garibaldi, having conquered the Bourbon Kingdom of the Two Sicilies, surrendered it to Victor Emmanuel II with the famous handshake at Teano in 1860. Leading figures in the Liberal movement, who had guided the process of unification elsewhere in the peninsula, strove to understand the territories the new kingdom had unexpectedly acquired, thereby laying the foundations for an intellectual tradition that became known as *meridionalismo*. This came to combine disciplines such as agronomy, economics, geography and sociology in order to explain the peculiarities of the South in relation to the rest of the country. The observations of the first *meridionalisti*— writers such as Franchetti, Sonnino, Villari and Turiello—were built upon by early twentieth-century scholars from a variety of ideological formations—for example the Liberal economist Nitti, the Catholic social reformer Sturzo and the Socialist thinker Salvemini. They used their analyses to develop diverse agendas for addressing the so-called 'Southern problem'—the underdevelopment of the South in comparison to the North.[1]

The discourses of *meridionalismo* exercised a great hold over subsequent historiography. The accounts by the early *meridionalisti* of their journeys of inquiry into the South and their experiences of its prefectures provided historians with a ready-made set of primary sources, all the more valuable given the overall scarcity of reliable data. Furthermore, *meridionalismo* established a critical framework through which to approach Southern history. Historical analysis focused on the causes of 'the Southern problem', employing explanations centred either on the lack of physical resource endowments in the South (poor soil, scarcity of water supplies, etc.), or upon the absence of such 'human' qualities as entrepreneurial and civic spirit amongst the Southern populace.

The enduring contrast between the Northern and Southern economies was explored within the conceptual framework of what has been called 'dualism'—the existence of two apparently separate economies side by side within the same state. Scholars contended over the extent and nature of the connection between the two, taking a range of positions: for instance, there were those who asserted that industrial development in Northern Italy had been based on an expropriation of the resources and potential of the *Mezzogiorno*, and others who replied that self-generated growth in the North had been held back by the 'ball and chain' of the Southern economy. Debate over the extent to which development in one region had been constrained (both economically and as a result of political choices) by subordination to the needs of the other dominated the historiography of the *Mezzogiorno* in the decades that followed the fall of Fascism.[2]

In the 1980s important new scholarship about the South appeared. Although acknowledging the powerful insights of individual *meridionalisti*, authors began challenging the premises of *meridionalismo*, arguing that it contained an inherent risk of distorting the realities of the *Mezzogiorno* because of its project of interpreting the South through implicit comparison with the North. A consequence of this was that, instead of emphasizing the dynamics of historical change within the South, *meridionalismo* highlighted the region's lack of dynamism compared to the rest of the country. The image of the *Mezzogiorno* that emerged from such analyses was of an unchanging, backward world, so that, as Piero Bevilacqua put it, the history of the South was reduced to the history of the Southern problem while Italian history was made elsewhere.[3] Furthermore, the revisionists argued, in contrasting South with North, *meridionalismo* suggested a spurious uniformity within the *Mezzogiorno*, implying that the entire area shared a similar set of characteristics that accounted for its underdevelopment. In this way a homogeneous, backward 'South' was constructed from the very different regions that had made up the Bourbon Kingdom.[4]

The appearance of histories of southern regions in the multi-volume history of Italy published by Einaudi in the second half of the 1980s underlined this diversity. Each volume brought together a number of contributors, many of them younger researchers who located their work within the context of international debates on theory and method, in contrast to the more politically determined approaches of an older, established, generation of scholars. It was their experience of editing the volume on Calabria in the Einaudi series that led to Piero Bevilacqua and Augusto Placanica to set up a new institute for the collaborative study of the *Mezzogiorno*, IMES, the Istituto Meridionale di Storia e Scienze Sociali, founded in 1986.[5] Its journal, *Meridiana*, became the standard-bearer for new approaches to the study of the South. It deliberately reached out to a wider public beyond the academic community, and regularly included policy makers and representatives of interested private and public institutions among its contributors, while also developing educational materials for schools.

These developments took place in the context of a broader renewal within Italian historiography that began with the belated arrival of the 'new social history', the breaking down of disciplinary boundaries such as those between history and anthropology, and an eagerness to insert the Italian case into comparative debates. This stimulated an innovative wave of historical production with the appearance of highly focused monographs which frequently challenged the generalizations of older texts. Many drew upon the so-called methodology of *microstoria*—an attempt to capture a 'holistic' picture of human interrelationships, which, of necessity, favoured the intensive study of a single episode, enterprise, family or, above all, community. These micro-analyses explored the cultural explanations of patterns of human interaction proposed by anthropology in preference to the 'scientific' representations of these offered by demographic and economic analysis. Instead of privileging class relations in their readings of the past, *microstoria* enabled social historians to focus their attention upon the role of such phenomena as brokerage networks and family forms in the functioning of society.[6]

A crucial contribution to this rejuvenation of Italian historiography was the foundation of new journals such as *Quaderni Storici* in the 1970s and *Passato e Presente* a decade later. These drew their inspiration from international models, such as those of *Annales* and *Past and Present*, eschewing the close links to political subcultures that characterized older titles such as the Marxist *Studi Storici*.[7] Individual publishers also played their part in this renewal; for example Carmine Donzelli, who moved from Einaudi to the Venetian publishers Marsilio in 1989, commissioned many pioneering historical studies for them, before founding his own eponymous publishing house in Rome.

Much of the best new writing was on the *Mezzogiorno*. The approaches adopted by these new authors were again interdisciplinary and innovative—game theory, network analysis, and 'postmodernist' techniques of deconstruction were all used as tools to analyse the South in an exchange that has involved, *inter alia* anthropologists, economists, historians and political scientists. This scholarship contained as many variations in approach and analysis as that of the *meridionalisti* themselves, and is still far from developing a consensus about the history of the *Mezzogiorno*. Rather, the common element in this revisionism was the recognition of the dangers occasioned by thinking about the South within the confines of a 'Southern problem'. As one leading revisionist polemically put it, the need was to analyse the '*Mezzogiorno* without *meridionalismo*'.[8]

The new literature rejected explanations of the South that invoked 'backwardness' or the failure of its inhabitants to appreciate their best interests, regarding these notions as products of vulgarized *meridionalismo*. Instead, scholars stressed that the socioeconomic structures of the various regions of the *Mezzogiorno* stemmed from a set of 'rational' responses to human (e.g. societal) and physical (e.g. climatic) factors. These structures evolved over time, in response to changing conditions, and could not, therefore, be explained away by historians as relics of a previous age.

Nowhere have these concerns been more evident than in the reappraisals of the Southern economy. The writings of the early *meridionalisti* depicted great estates (*latifondi*) whose absentee owners rented them out to generate sufficient income to support their social status, rather than farm them directly with the intention of maximizing profits. Instead of improving the land, they let it out to middlemen (*gabellotti*) who then sublet it in small parcels to peasant cultivators on short-term rents, calculated (and often payable) as a proportion of the crop. Consequently these so-called *coloni* were encouraged to seek the immediate returns offered by cereals, and in particular wheat, rather than invest in planting more appropriate 'Medi-terranean' crops such as citrus fruits and olives, upon which returns would be greater but would have to be deferred until the trees reached maturity. The early *meridionalisti* such as Sonnino and Franchetti compared this unfavourably to their native Tuscany, where, they maintained, stable sharecropping arrangements made improvements possible because of the direct interest of both landowner and tenant in profit maximization. By contrast they portrayed the organization of the *latifondi* as inherently backward and more feudal than capitalist, with the lack of investment in the land rendering economic development impossible.[9]

The new generation of scholars argued that this presentation ignored the diversity of the Southern economy, or, more accurately, economies. While it may have come close to describing the situation in western Sicily (the subject of the inquiries of Sonnino and Franchetti), it had little relevance to the cattle-rearing *latifondi* of Lazio, for example, and ignored the fact that many of the mainland *latifondi*, if not directly farmed by the landlords themselves, were certainly managed by resident agents, rather than let and then sublet in the Sicilian manner. Furthermore there were a great variety of tenancy forms, and assorted parcels of land were often let to the same peasant under different conditions. Viniculture, for example, was promoted through longer-lasting contracts, which rewarded the tenant for improvements made to the land.[10]

The desire to transform fields into vineyards, most evident in the 1870s when this sector resisted the general fall in agricultural prices caused by the influx of imports from both the New World and the Far East, was also indicative of a responsiveness to market conditions that went unremarked in the older literature. The existence of a substantial sector of highly commercialized agriculture in the coastal zones of the *Mezzogiorno* where the almond, citrus and olive groves best flourished was, claimed the revisionists, largely ignored. Over the course of the nineteenth century the land employed in this manner generated some of the highest returns in Europe. Capital investment was concentrated in commerce, attracted by the surety of high profits to be made in exporting primary 'Mediterranean' produce, rather than in manufacturing or in the development of the interior *latifondi*. There was, then, an explanation based on economic rationality and profit maximization for the apparent underdevelopment of the *Mezzogiorno*.[11]

Some revisionists went beyond this to argue that the *latifondo* itself was a flexible enterprise, capable both of responding to the market through the combination of crops and tenancy forms described above, and of providing protection from it. This latter feature was particularly necessary given the commercial sector was highly exposed to events in its overseas markets. Any changes in these could seriously affect profitability, as occurred when the impact of the agricultural depression was intensified in the 1880s by the introduction of protectionist tariffs and the outbreak of the trade war with France. This pointed to the need to understand the concentration on wheat production for domestic consumption that the *meridionalisti* highlighted, in the particular context of the times in which they were writing.

This new emphasis on the 'rationality' of the *latifondo* was taken furthest by Marta Petrusewicz, who argued that *latifondismo* was a distinct form of agrarian enterprise, neither feudal or capitalist, which had evolved in harmony with overall conditions in the South, enjoying its heyday between the 1820s and the 1880s.[12] Basing her analysis on the largest *latifondo* in Calabria, she argued that as well as representing the most effective way of exploiting the resources of the lands of the interior, estates were also able to maintain a moral legitimacy in the eyes of their resident labourers and tenants who, until the 1880s, enjoyed more stable long-term relationships with the enterprise, bolstered by the extension of various privileges, than was previously acknowledged.

Petrusewicz was accused of misrepresenting the dependency relationships between the estate and its employees by describing them in terms of a 'moral economy' based on shared expectations of behaviour, and by extending the conclusions she reached in what was essentially a *microstoria* of one unique *latifondo* to the institution as a whole.[13] In her essay accounting for the demise of '*latifondismo*' which opens this collection, she clarifies her ideas about the nature of the latifundia system arguing that it was external pressures, including those created by the new Liberal state, that forced on the *latifondo* a capitalist 'modernization', which failed to deliver either the economic success or the social peace that *lati-*

fondismo had generated. The *meridionalisti*, however, had read this crisis as proof of the inherent 'backwardness' of the *latifondo*.

New writings on other aspects of the *Mezzogiorno* shared this stress on the need for historical specificity. Just as the *latifondo* of the Restoration period was rehabilitated, so too were aspects of the performance of the Bourbon state. Recent histories have argued that the restored monarchy did not simply turn the clock back on the reforms that took place during the French occupation, but adopted and adapted these to its own ends: for example, the Bourbon state's promotion of environmental and infrastructural improvement programmes (abandoned by the post-unification Liberal regime on the grounds that such initiatives were solely the responsibility of the individual landowner) has now been recognized.[14]

The key feature of these reinterpretations of the Bourbon period was the stress laid upon the emergence of a new, rural, bourgeoisie encouraged by the removal of restrictions on land sales by the Bourbon regime, following the anti-feudal land sales instigated by the French occupants of the mainland *Mezzogiorno* in 1806 and the British in Sicily in 1812. As well as forming a more dynamic class of landowners—such as the Barracco family, proprietors of the *latifondo* studied by Petrusewicz—this new social stratum found its political aspirations accommodated in the new local councils, *comuni*, that replaced the previous feudal institutions. Although the *comuni* were subject to the control of *intendenti* who repre-sented the central Bourbon state in the provinces (adapting the model developed in Napoleonic France) they were granted a considerable degree of autonomy over their affairs. Con-sequently there was greater scope for the development of political activity than was apparent in the damning critiques of public administration penned by the original *meridionalisti*.

However, according to Paolo Pezzino's chapter in this book, the newly empowered bourgeoisie did not so much overthrow the existing nobility as merge with it at the level of the *comune* in order to resist the authority of the central state. Rather than being a tool for political transformation, the *comune* was used as a defensive weapon by provincial élites. Unable to confront this entrenched localism, the centre was forced to reach accommodations with it. This pattern persisted after the advent of the Liberal regime as the local élites continued to use the *comuni* as a bastion against the incursions of the new state, leading disillusioned Liberals to sanction the virtual civil war that took place in the South in the 1860s. While the army was able to maintain military control in the *Mezzogiorno* (albeit at a far greater cost to human life than that paid for Unification), the state's attempts to transplant liberal democracy to the South fell on stony ground. Clientelism and corruption came to be thought of as characteristic of Southern politics.

For many analysts this was indicative of an almost genetic 'backwardness' in Southern society, which had failed to develop those civic virtues necessary to promote good government, notably that of association in pursuit of common goals other than the pursuit of immediate private profit. While the early *meridionalisti* tended to view this as indicative of the lack of independence of the bulk of the populace from the landowners (thus perversely justifying the restriction of the franchise to the very élite who exercised power over others), other interpretations of the so-called *scioltezza*, or absence of social bonds between individuals, have focused on what the anthropologist Edward Banfield famously dubbed the 'amoral familism' of the Southern population, that is the privileging of the nuclear family network to the virtual exclusion of any other.[15]

Recently, Robert Putnam, the American political scientist, suggested that contemporary differences in the level of performance of regional government in the North and South of Italy reflect the prevalence of 'horizontal', democratic types of association in the former (such as choirs and mutual aid societies) and 'vertical' networks of hierarchy and deference in the latter (embodied in the church and the *mafia*).[16] He traced the roots of this difference back to the twelfth century, contrasting the emergence of republican city states in the North and Centre in the absence of a dominant single power, with the strong central state created at the expense of local autonomy in the Norman kingdom of the South. The Northern city states created the condition in which a virtuous cycle for formation of 'social capital' could take root, as the emergence of many competing 'horizontal' forms of association in the spaces between the individual and the state enabled a civic tradition based on mutual trust and democratic engagement to be established. This legitimized the principle that an impartial authority (the state) should administer public goods, be these physical (e.g. water supplies), or abstract (e.g. justice). The South, however, was stuck in a vicious cycle in which the strategy of clientelism provided the only response to the concentration of public goods in the hands of a state in which feudalism, autocracy and bureaucracy had combined to produce a hierarchical power over which individuals could not aspire to exercise any form of collective control.

Putnam's then, was another analysis of the South that essentially consisted of noting the absence of features found in the North, once more portraying the *Mezzogiorno* through a Northern prism. Similarly his argument that the South had been stuck in a 'stable equilibrium' since at least the eleventh century, apparently suggesting that the best route to improved democratic performance was to get a better medieval past, demonstrated precisely the slippage from historical specificity to a historical characterization against which much of the new analysis of the *Mezzogiorno* has been directed. Indeed, Putnam's view of the Northern past was equally partial, as it was predicted on a presumption that a historical memory of civic engagement survived from the demise of the city states in the fourteenth century, through centuries of foreign and authoritarian regimes, to successfully re-emerge after Unification. It was also notable that Putnam used associationism in the late nineteenth century to predict the pattern of civic engagement after the 1970s, thus ignoring the fact that popular Fascism, with its predilection for dissolving 'subversive' municipalities, was also a Northern phenomenon.[17]

Putnam did accept that clientelism and familism formed a rational behavioural strategy in situations where a civic community was lacking, however.[18] It is defining the precise nature of this rationality that has informed much of the best new writing on the problems of *malgoverno* ('misgovernment', 'neglect') in the *Mezzogiorno*. Here there is a striking parallel between the medieval city states described by Putnam, in which citizenship and its benefits were largely restricted to an élite that was a fusion of the nobility and the emergent bourgeoisie, and the recent portrayals of the Bourbon and Liberal *comuni* as institutions in which much the same process occurred. Electors and councillors contended between themselves over such issues as which forms of revenue collection to employ and on what the monies raised should be spent, reaching decisions that favoured the interests of the majority of the enfranchised electorate, but not necessarily the majority of those over whom the institution ruled. The prefects who exercised authority over the municipalities in the name of the Liberal state at times sought to protect the interests of those without a vote, but, like their predecessors, the *intendenti*, they were usually forced to compromise with established local interests in order to compensate for the lack of legitimacy enjoyed by the central authorities at any social level.[19]

Thus there continued to be a caste monopoly of public goods. Within the *comuni* this caste was extended into the various intermediary social strata known as the *ceti medi* (agents, doctors, lawyers, etc.), whose enfranchisement did not produce a social renewal so much as a consolidation of a clientelism that was able to transcend class boundaries. In these circumstances it was in an individual's interest to construct the kinds of hierarchical connections that would allow him some access to the resources monopolized by the élite. Analysis of the patronage networks that prevailed in Southern politics at the end of the nineteenth century demonstrated that individual voters were rewarded, as much as coerced, into casting their votes for the appropriate candidate at local and national elections.[20] Furthermore, if electors believed that a potential deputy lacked a sufficiently 'big name' to deliver benefits in the form of favours from the state, they could force a change of candidate upon the local notable at the head of the clientelistic chain. Even after the franchise was extended in the 1880s, it continued to be the case that clientelistic comportment offered the individual elector the best form of return on his vote. The state was not seen as an impartial arbiter, but as a resource to which one gained access through connections.

In his chapter on nineteenth century Naples Paolo Macry describes how the distribution of what he describes as 'fake goods', that is goods that were not meant to be sold, distorted the public administration of that city so that instead of presiding over the application of universal norms, it simply brokered individual favours. His account of the various redistributive circles that characterized the Neapolitan economy highlights an essential feature of entrepreneurship in the South: a preference for activities involving mediation and brokerage over the actual production of goods. This commercial vocation was often missed by accounts of Italian 'dualism' that contrasted the industrial North with the agrarian South, even though concentrating on trade was a wholly rational response to the opportunities offered to contractors by a Bourbon state that frequently farmed out the monopolies it created.[21] Such forms of profit maximization, however, inevitably resulted in investing in the very poverty that has been seen as characteristic of Southern underdevelopment. Macry uncovers the various circuits by which money passed through the hands of usurers, credit banks and gamblers drawn from all social classes, uniting them in the expectation of a return on their stake that could not be achieved through other forms of activity.

No group was more skilled at this time than the criminal organization known as the *camorra* which, one of its members boasted, could conjure 'gold from lice'. This was achieved through the strategy of selling a social good in short supply, trust, in the form of protection against the lack of trust that the activities of the *camorra* generated. Macry's explanation of organized crime as essentially a business activity is one that is shared by recent writing on the other criminal organizations in the South, the Calabrian *'ndrangheta* and the Sicilian *mafia*. The sociopolitical analyses of these phenomena that portrayed them variously as forms of primitive social protest, informal social control, or a simple construct of the state, have been replaced by a new school of scholarship that affirms the reality of an organization that concentrated upon the commercial opportunities created by the absence of legitimate sources of public authority.[22] In these writings the violent entrepreneurs of older interpretations have been replaced by entrepreneurs of violence who sell the commodity of trust not as agents for a particular class or stratum, but as autonomous 'businessmen' acting 'rationally' in their own interests.

The *mafia*, of course, looms large in the popular perception of the South, along with other, essentially negative, cultural stereotypes. A key feature of the new writing on the *Mezzogiorno* has been the preparedness to utilize methods often associated with 'postmodernism' to analyse the ways in which the South has been 'imagined'. Gabriella Gribaudi's chapter concerns the ways in which Southern identities have bee developed and reinforced through the reception of the work of the *meridionalisti*. While these writers were themselves guilty of exaggerating certain features of the region over others, it is the selectiveness with which aspects of their interpretations were appropriated to reinforce preconceived notions of difference that has characterized the problem of representation. Gribaudi points out, for example, that Banfield's concept of 'amoral familism' mentioned above, was, in fact, a very specific description of the behaviour of nuclear families in the village in the Basilicata where he performed his fieldwork, yet in the long-running debate over the book, it was widely read as being characteristic of extended and paternalistic family forms wrongly assumed to be characteristic of the South. A scientific study was appropriated to justify a stultifying stereotype, the pervasiveness of which was demonstrated by its absorbtion by Southerners themselves.

This, suggests Gribaudi, should alert us to a central problem in relation to representation and reality, namely that a weak concept may easily come to inhabit the identities constructed for it by a more powerful force. The messages sent to the Southerners by the Left's insistence that salvation lay in a peasant alliance with the vanguard forces of the Northern proletariat, the Fascist rhetoric that spoke of the modernization of the North and the ruralization of the South, and the state interventionalist policies pursued by the Christian Democrats through the post-war Cassa per il Mezzogiorno, were all ones that situated the South in a dependency relationship, characterizing it as incapable of generating its own renewal. Acceptance of such an identity helps to explain such events as the virtual insurrection in Eboli in May 1974 in protest against the failure of the state to direct a new factory to the town.[23]

John Dickie's chapter concentrates on the ways in which the need to construct an Italian identity in the decades following Unification shaped the representations of the South in this period. Although the Liberal regime was at times able to use the South as an 'Other' against which to posit an Italian identity, it had also to incorporate the South within such an identity, and persuade both Northerners and Southerners that such an identity could be shared. It therefore mattered that the execution of a brigand be carried out in the correct manner, as this was intended to convey a set of messages about the codes of conduct in a civilized society to constituencies that stretched from the enfranchised élite of Italian citizens to the common peasants who had yet to be integrated into the newly created Kingdom. An acceptance of the possibility that the two identities could coexist was fundamental to the construction of the South as an uncivilized, almost mystical locale in which there none the less existed innate 'Italian' characteristics. Such representations of the *Mezzogiorno* were common amongst Southern intellectuals such as Nicefero, who sought to gain it the benefit of a civilizing yoke.

Dickie argues that by thinking about 'the South', the enfranchised citizenry could address the challenges to the (or, rather, their) nation itself. The construction of Crispi's 'Sicilian-ness' and the stress placed on the picturesque qualities of the Southern poor by 'national' newspapers and magazines for the enfranchised middle classes should be read in conjunction with contemporary concerns raised by episodes such as the violent protests of the Sicilian *fasci* (peasant and workers' groups) in 1894. His emphasis on context returns us to the importance of historical specificity that characterizes so much of the recent work on the *Mezzogiorno*.

This collection concludes with Fulvio Cammarano's chapter on the question of nation-building in the political arena. He argues that while the Liberal élite sought to legitimize the new

Kingdom through the institutionalization of its political structures, they dared not permit the politicization of the nation, that is the development of national forms of political expression among all Italians, for fear that this might undermine that very legitimacy. While this was clearly a limitation that was held to apply to the South in the immediate post-Unification period, what is striking about Cammarano's analysis is that so many of the politicizing challenges to the State—the organized politics of the Socialist, Catholic and Nationalist movements, for instance—were products of the municipal politics of the North. Indeed, Giolitti, the Piedmontese statesman who dominated parliamentary politics in the first two decades of the twentieth century, famously owed his position to a majority built on the support of Southern deputies (the so-called *ascari*). It was the trade-offs, corruption and outright ballot-rigging involved in sustaining this position that were Salvemini's targets in his attacks on 'the myth of good government' during the Giolittian era.[24]

Just as 'the South' was not merely an 'Other' constructed to play the role of a distorted mirror image to an imagined 'Italy', so 'the North' cannot be presented as a synonym for 'the Nation'. Indeed one of the most important implications of those approaches, which investigate the 'making of the meaning' of the *Mezzogiorno*, is the need to explore the conceptual content of these other labels as well. This was recognized by the editors of *Meridiana* when they commissioned a volume specifically addressing *La questione settentrionale* (The Northern Problem), while Donzelli, publishers of Bevilacqua's *Breve storia dell'Italia meridionale* (Brief History of Southern Italy) (an attempted synthesis of the new writing on the *Mezzogiorno*), recently brought out a *Breve storia dell'Italia settentrionale* (Brief History of Northern Italy) whose starting point was, once again, the diversity of historical forms and experiences in the territories surrounding the River Po.[25]

These developments were not just the product of ongoing debates in historiography: they too must be set in the contemporary context of the rise of a Northern federalist/separatist party in the 1980s, which played a fundamental role in unravelling the political structures of the Italian Republic in the 1990s. The renewal of interest in the history of the South predated the rise of the Northern League, so that IMES (with its strategy of reaching out beyond academic circles) and many other intellectuals outside its ranks were well positioned to engage with the propositions the League advanced.[26] Whatever their doubts about the 'Southern problem' as a conceptual tool for historical analysis, these scholars remained convinced of the moral and political legitimacy of the contemporary 'Southern question'.[27] Indeed, the stereotyping of Southerners in the League's discourses provided a perfect present-day example of utilizing 'the South' as a way of thinking about 'national' problems that permeated all Italian public life, not just that of the *Mezzogiorno*.[28]

It is the interplay between the analysis of the material and symbolic spheres that has fundamentally altered the historiography of the *Mezzogiorno* in particular and Italy in general. It is no longer plausible to present an undifferentiated analysis of 'the South' that operates on the premise of a 'backwardness' that is the product of a constant set of characteristics. Recently even the production of the official statistics that appeared to define so clearly the differences between the North and South of Italy was analysed as an act of construction that 'far from merely reflecting a state of things' as the positivists responsible for their collection intended, 'established the kind of "comparativist" approach that has characterized the debate on the "southern question" since its origins'.[29]

Yet the author of this study made clear that 'by drawing attention to the contribution of statistics to the making of the "two Italies" ', she was 'not denying the existence of differences in the texture of economic, social and political life within Italy'.[30] It is important that these necessary rereadings of Southern history do not lend themselves to a new historical construction of the South that simply inverts previous negative images. To ensure against this it will be necessary not only to acknowledge the flexibility of the *latifondo* system in responding to specific moments and circumstances, which was for so long ignored, but to remember that this was indeed achieved through maintaining the low labour costs that were so often remarked upon. Similarly accounts of the 'rational' behaviour of individuals within the political economy of both the *comune* and the city will still have to take as their point of departure the real scarcity of 'public goods' in the South. Only then can we move beyond explanations of the history of the South that focus on stereotypical portrayals of class conflict, endemic corruption and organized criminality to ones that highlight the mutual dependency of proprietors and workers, as well as politicians and electors, and the very different forms of social legitimacy that these engendered. The value of the new historiography lies not in a denial of the particularities of the history of the *Mezzogiorno*, but its preparedness to rethink ways of explaining this.

NOTES

1. Gabriella Gribaudi's chapter in this volume contains a detailed discussion of both the work and reception of the *meridionalisti*.
2. The most valuable recent analysis of Italian dualism is L. Cafagna, *Dualismo e sviluppo nella storia d'Italia* (Venice, 1989).
3. P. Bevilacqua, *Breve storia dell'Italia meridionale dall'Ottocento ad oggi* (Rome, 1993), vii.
4. Many of these positions are captured in the 'Presentazione' of *Meridiana*, published in the first edition of the journal, 1 (1987), 9–15.
5. P. Bevilacqua and A. Placanica, eds, *La Calabria (Storia dell'Italia. Storia delle regioni dall'Unità ad oggi)* (Turin, 1985). Other key volumes to appear were M. Aymard and G. Giarrizzo, eds, *La Sicilia* (Turin, 1987); L. Masella and B. Salvemini, eds, *La Puglia* (1989); P. Macry and P. Villani, eds, *La Campania* (Turin, 1990).
6. For recent developments in Italian historiography see J.A. Davis, 'Remapping Italy's Path to the Twentieth Century', *Journal of Modern History*, 66 (1994), 291–330. One of the most important manifestos in favour of *microstoria* was E. Grendi, 'Micro-analisi e storia sociale', *Quaderni storici*, 35 (1977) 501–20. The relationships between social anthropology and history and Italian and Anglo-American scholarships are discussed in P. Filipucci, 'Anthropological Perspectives on Culture in Italy', in D. Forgacs and R. Lumley, eds, *Italian Cultural Studies* (Oxford, 1996), 52–71.
7. On trends in historical journals see J. Morris, 'Italian Journals: A User's Guide', *Contemporary European History*, I, 3 (1992), 89–97.
8. G. Giarrizzo, *Mezzogiorno senza meridionalismo. La Sicilia, lo sviluppo, il potere* (Venice, 1992). Giarrizzo makes his case most explicitly in the introduction to the book, pp. ix–xxxi.
9. L. Franchetti and S. Sonnino, *Inchiesta in Sicilia* (Florence, 1876). For an account of Sicilian conditions that largely operates along these lines

see D. Mack-Smith, 'The Latifundia in Modern Sicilian History', in *Transactions of the Royal Historical Society* (1965), 85–124.

10. S. Lupo, 'I proprietari terrieri nel Mezzogiorno' in P. Bevilacqua, ed., *Storia dell'agricoltura italiana in età contemporanea*, II (Venice, 1990), 105–49. On the variety of tenure systems in the South see J. Cohen and F. Galasso, 'The Economics of Tenancy in Early Twentieth-century Southern Italy', *Economic History Review*, XLVII, 3 (1994), 585–600.

11. This case was made by P. Bevilacqua in first issue of *Meridiana*: 'Il Mezzogiorno nel mercato internazionale', *Meridiana*, 1 (1987), 17–46. It forms the basis of much of the authors' subsequent *Breve storia dell'Italia meridonale*. One excellent account of the commercial sector in citrus is S. Lupo, *Il giardino degli aranci: il mondo degli agrumi nella storia del Mezzogiorno* (Venice, 1990).

12. M. Petrusewicz, *Latifondo* (Venice, 1989), now translated as *Latifundium: Moral Economy and Material Life in a European Periphery* (Ann Arbor, 1996).

13. See the letters to the *Times Literary Supplement* by G. dal Vivo on 8 November and 27 December 1991; and the criticisms in G. Montrini, *Gli uomini del re* (Rome, 1996), ix.

14. C. d'Elia, *Bonifiche e stato nel Mezzogiorno, 1815–1869* (Naples, 1995).

15. E. Banfield, *The Moral Basis of Backward Society* (Illinois, 1958).

16. R. Putnam, *Making Democracy Work. Civic Traditions in Modern Italy* (Princeton, 1993).

17. For a caustic critique of Putnam see S. Lupo, 'Usi e abusi del passato: le radici dell'Italia di Putnam', *Meridiana*, 18 (1993). The issues raised by the book are well discussed in J. Bloomfield 'The "Civic" in Europe', *Contemporary European History*, 4/2 (July 1995), 224–32.

18. R. Putnam, *Making Democracy Work*, (1994), 177.

19. R. Romanelli, *Il commando impossibile* (Bologna, 1988).

20. L. Musella, *Individui, amici, clienti. Relazioni personali e circuiti politici in Italia meridionale tra Otto e Novecento* (Bologna, 1994).

21. J.A. Davis, *Merchants, Monopolists and Contractors: A Study of Economic Activity in Bourbon Naples, 1815–1860* (New York, 1981).

22. Contrast the interpretations of the *mafia* advanced in such analyses as E. Hobsbawm, *Primitive Rebels* (Manchester, 1959); A. Blok, *The Mafia of a Sicilian Village* (Oxford, 1985); and C. Duggan, *Fascism and the Mafia* (New Haven, 1989); with those of P. Pezzino, *Una certa reciprocità di favori* (Milan, 1990); S. Lupo, *Storia della mafia dalle origine ai giorni nostri* (Rome, 1993); and D. Gambetta, *The Sicilian Mafia. The Business of Private Protection* (Cambridge, Mass., 1993).

23. G. Gribaudi, *A Eboli* (Venice, 1990), 3–13.

24. See G. Salvemini, *Scritti sulla questione meridionale (1896–1955)* (Turin, 1955). This theme was subsequently explored in M. Salvadori, *Il mito del buongoverno. La questione meridionale da Cavour a Gramsci* (Turin, 1960).

25. *La questione settentrionale*, special issue of *Meridiana*, 16 (1993); M. Meriggi, *Breve storia dell'Italia settentrionale* (Rome, 1996).

26. See, for example, L. Cafagna, *Nord e Sud. Non fare a pezzi l'unità d'Italia* (Venice, 1994), which utilizes a review of recent historiographical production on the South (that often opposes the positions adopted by Bevilacqua and *Meridiana*) to this end.

27. See P. Bevilacqua, 'New and Old in the Southern Question', *Modern Italy*, 1, n. 2 (1996), 81–92.
28. For a subtle interpretation of Northern League discourse see A. Cento Bull, 'Ethnicity, Racism and the Northern League', in C. Levy, ed., *Italian Regionalism* (Oxford, 1996), 171–87.
29. S. Patriaca, *Numbers and Nationhood* (Cambridge, 1996), 239–40.
30. Ibid, 239.

2

The Demise of *Latifondismo*

Marta Petrusewicz

Latifondismo was a system of economic production and social relations that came into being during the revolutionary and Napoleonic period and dominated the agricultural world of the mainland part of the Kingdom of the Two Sicilies for the best part of the nineteenth century.[1] At the centre of this system was the *latifondo*, the large landed estates that exercised hegemony over an immense territory consisting of plains, hills and mountains, towns, villages and forests, inhabited by a population of several thousands. In this territory the *latifondo* (Latin: *latifundium*) was the main, if not only, employer; it was the dispenser of protection, the source of credit, and the mediator enabling access to legal and medical services and to the institutions of the state. It also had control of the use of force.

Latifondismo was neither feudal nor capitalist; it was a mixture—a mixture of subsistence and market-oriented production, of cereal cultivation and husbandry, of the most modern and most primitive agricultural methods, of industry and agriculture, of monetary wages and retribution in kind, of local and international markets, of modern management combined with sharecropping and land assignments. The most remarkable characteristic of this system was its stability. Its universe was poor, illiterate and malaric, but not impoverished in its wealth of collective security and density of networks and exchanges. Its moral economy was geared to the satisfaction of broadly understood needs rather than to maximizing profits. It was rational, in the sense described by Alexandr Chayanov,[2] in that it offered different but equally desired advantages to the latifondisti on the one side and to the labourers on the other. The landowners realized huge savings in labour disciplining, supervision and training, in monetary expenditure in wages, in costs of raw materials, maintenance and transportation, as well as in the costs of reproduction of their lifestyle. The labourers enjoyed a lifetime guarantee of employment for all the members of the family, protection and assistance in times of material and social need, and the possibility of maintaining their peasant status based on access to land, control over the apprenticeship of children and over the exercise and transmission of their ancestral know-how. Both sides partook in a social pact of, admittedly unequal, exchange of loyalty for security as both had stakes in perpetuating the old paternalistic–patriarchal order.

Latifondismo ended at the close of the nineteenth century in a wave of economic transformations and social unrest, giving birth to a new capitalist *latifondo*, an infamous protagonist of the *Mezzogiorno*'s history in the first half of the twentieth century. In this chapter I shall examine the mechanisms of *latifondismo*'s demise, taking as my case study the fate of the largest Calabrian *latifondo*, that of the Barracco family.

The decline of the *latifondo* economy

In the last two decades of the nineteenth century the Barracco *latifundium*, long considered the largest, the strongest and the richest in the Kingdom, began to show signs of decline. It became evident in the production of all quality commodities traditionally destined for distant markets such as grain, cheese, fine wood, olive oil and liquorice.[3] Wheat and rye outputs fell off steadily and by the turn of the century had reached levels that were not only four times less than in the 1860s boom but two times less than in the first two decades of the *latifondo*'s existence. By 1898 the number of sheep had dwindled to less than half the figures for 1862 and 1867; the number of goats was all of seven times less. Average production of sheep's milk cheese in the period 1887–1903 was three to four times less than in the 1850s and 1860s and ten times less than in 1835–43, that of *caciocavallo* cheese and fine wool was halved. The same happened to olive oil and liquorice, typical Mediterranean products thought to be insensitive to market fluctuations. Oil output remained steadily high up to 1887— the portentous year of bumper harvests and protective tariffs—then began to fall, reaching an all-century low in 1899. In the last years of the century liquorice output plummeted, too.

This decline was taking place in the context of the general crisis in European agriculture. The United States, where Reconstruction was in full swing, flooded the European markets with fine wheat from the virgin lands of the Midwest, grown and transported at costs so low as to cause an unprecedented drop in prices: they fell by more than half between 1873 and 1895. For a variety of reasons, in Italy the full brunt of the crisis was not felt until 1881, but then it became omnipresent: small farms went bankrupt, wages dropped, unemployment grew, property improvements were abandoned as well as marginal lands that had been brought into cultivation during the wheat-boom years. Farmers with sufficient strength and capital tried to pull through by converting from wheat to grapes, citrus fruit, olives and livestock, thereby augmenting the general confusion. In Calabria, too, the first wave of the crisis brought the small peasant proprietors to ruin and triggered an advance flow of emigration. Tenant farmers, who had signed high-rent leases in better days, were squeezed, and this precipitated a frantic race to plant citrus groves and vineyards.

The onset of the Great Depression, however, did not affect directly the *latifondo* economy, whose decline did not come till much later. According to one interpretation, the *latifondo*'s crisis was simply a belated repercussion of the so-called tenants' crisis: when leases came up for renewal, absentee landlords, who relied on rents collected by their agents, found themselves squeezed by the tenants' financial straits and forced to lower lease prices. This explanation, which makes sense when applied to the absentee *latifondismo*, risks measuring the whole South by a Sicilian yardstick. For the continental *latifondisti*—who stayed on the land managed their property themselves and made extensive use of hired labour—rent income was of secondary importance and, being paid mainly in kind, was not subject to inflation. The *latifondisti*'s economy was indeed shaken to its roots by the consequences of the Great Depression, but this had occurred through a complex interaction of different factors: price depression, the *latifondisti*'s new initiative and Italy's commercial policies.

Traditional reaction mechanisms

It seems reasonable to examine the *latifondo*'s reaction to the slump first through price analysis. After all, the *latifondo* was a business enterprise, whose 'rich' commodities—olive oil, sheep's-milk cheese, wheat, liquorice, fine wool and *cacio-cavallo* cheese—were sold in distant markets at prices determined by (and fluctuating with) those markets rather than by production costs. Hence its commercial production responded to changes in the wider market; any weakness in the latter was immediately transmitted to the producer and provoked adjustments in production.

But it is precisely the direction that these adjustments took, that distinguishes the *latifondo* from a 'true' capitalist enterprise. A 'true' capitalist enterprise would react to market fluctuations by turning toward the product that sold best and cutting back on the less successful ones, with all the predictable consequences for market equilibrium, prices, tenant farmers, marginal lands, commodity balance, and so on. In brief, it would behave according to the classic mechanism whereby the market governs farm production; a mechanism that presupposes unlimited flexibility in the placement of production factors, capacity to mobilize or demobilize reserves at will, and maximization of profit as the ultimate goal of production.

It was not so in the *latifondo*. Although its production was predominantly market-oriented and its products sold at market prices, the *latifondo*'s was not a 'true' market economy, but one whose profits were realized in the market. In the *latifondo* straight selling was more important than the calculation of competitive edges. Given the operation's low production costs on the one hand, and the permanent gap between local and world prices (with the latter consistently higher) on the other, the owner's interest lay always in selling, preferably in distant markets, at the going price, whatever it might be. There was always a profit to be made, even when prices were low; in fact, the *latifondo*'s yearly accounts always closed with a net profit.[4] There existed, of course, a non-remunerative price threshold but for *latifondo* products it was quite low; in fact some profit always showed in the yearly accounts.

The *latifondista*'s decisions about production depended only minimally on market phenomena. Indeed, in the *latifondo*'s heyday, that dependence was often inverse: output volume decreased between 1835 and 1839, when prices were rising, and between 1855 and 1859, when they were very high. Conversely, the Barraccos made their most aggressive and intense efforts at land accumulation (with consequent growth in grain output) in two periods of market slump: the post-Napoleonic years and the so-called mid-century crisis.

For the *latifondista* the goal of production was to assure consumption, maintain his social standing and perpetuate the whole system of social relations, not to maximize profit. However committed to rational administration and modernization, the *latifondista* was still a gentleman farmer, not an 'economizer'. Like most of the nineteenth-century European 'peripheral' landowners, the *latifondista* wanted, not money, but what money could buy—he was interested not in prices but in the terms of trade between the commodities he could sell and those he had to buy. His tendency was to increase production not so much when prices were high as when they were so low as to threaten his income. As long as revenues from his properties sufficed to meet his economic and social needs, he felt no need to act. Only incontrovertible evidence that market terms had worsened and that (if he hoped to maintain his standard of living and social status) losses would have to be made up by increasing aggregate output, could prompt him to take action. If in this case we can speak of market incentives to investment, they were, for the most part, negative: when market terms worsened, they set off a stimulus to compensate for losses by producing more.[5]

Thus, when in the 1880s Barraccos' revenues were threatened by lowering prices, it would have been natural for them to seek to increase output: either in the old way—avoiding cash outlays and using socially and economically cheaper methods to extend the scale of production—or by modernizing and mechanizing their operations, their practice in more recent decades. They did, indeed, attempt this traditional response, but it proved inadequate and unviable. In the years 1887–99 the correlation between prices and *latifondo* outputs became positive: grain wool and olive oil volumes declined significantly in agreement with the marked downswing in prices. It was a qualitatively new phenomenon, which begs an explanation.

The agricultural crisis and Italian trade policy

The explanation lies in a combination of factors. On the one hand, an effort at modernization undertaken in the third quarter of the nineteenth century, made the *latifondo* more market-sensitive. It consisted in shifting the balance from pasture towards cereal cultivation, from the 'natural' sector to the monetary basis, and in the growing specialization in 'rich' products for the Naples market, while neglecting alternative local outlets almost entirely. Although the *latifondo* could still sell cheap, it became more dependent on distant market demand and, for the first time, vulnerable to price fluctuations.

On the other hand, the commercial outlets were closing. In the last two decades of the century the Barraccos began to be hard-pressed to find outlets for their produce, an ever larger proportion of which no longer found its way to Naples. Commercialization ratio (quantities shipped to Naples as a percentage of total outputs) fell dramatically for all the export commodities: for sheep's-milk cheese, where it used to be 100 per cent or more (if the supply in any one year did not meet demand, an advance sale of the next year year's output would be 'bespoken'), it fell to an average of 80 per cent; for liquorice, which had no alternative outlet, it fell from 90 to 100 per cent to less than 30 per cent. Whereas in the past 35–40 per cent of the *latifondo*'s wheat was sold directly in Naples, and most of the remaining 60–65 per cent was taken up by large local traders, now the Naples market absorbed no more than a meagre fraction (3–5 per cent), while the large Calabrian traders either bought less or ceased to buy at all. Likewise oil, which for decades had followed a set pattern—75 per cent shipped to Naples, the remainder distributed by way of *minatici* (monthly allotments of fixed quantities of goods as a part of labour remuneration), gifts, and palace consumption, the occasional surpluses sold locally—now had a commercialization ratio reduced by a quarter, and the large local traders began to demand oranges instead.

Even those products sent to Naples did not necessarily find buyers; unsold stocks on hand in the Naples warehouse amounted to around 50 per cent of the quantities shipped. Even when the Barraccos were willing to sell at any price, the buyers were fewer and more demanding. Large Neapolitan traders—the Forquets, the Rouths, the Klentzes—once used to buy everything that reached Naples or Castellammare.[6] Now often the same houses—the Wolf Stolts, the Klentzes, the Langrafas, the Gervasis, the Savas, and the d'Amores—were buying one commodity only and that in limited quantity, while the local markets were too rigid to absorb the difference.

It was precisely the matter of market outlets, that the *latifondo* took the full force of the Great Depression. But that impact was neither direct nor was the main concern grain. On the contrary, in the early years of the Depression the fact that American wheat imports had driven Italian prices down seemed to play in favour of the *latifondisti*, as falling prices led to greater per capita consumption, with a consequent increase in aggregate demand.[7] At that time the *latifondo*'s output continued to find its way to one market niche or another, the wheat stopping in Naples, the oil, liquorice, and bergamot proceeding, with the aid of foreign traders, to the soap, perfume and pharmaceutical factories of Marseilles. Italy's exports of typical southern products remained satisfactory, while imports of competitive products were judged 'reasonable'. Hence, despite the price depression, the *latifondo* economy did well as long as Italy maintained a free-trade policy and continued to keep its doors open to commerce. The situation changed in 1887 with the introduction of protective tariffs.

It is now well established that the impact of protectionist legislation on Italy's trade in farm products was especially damaging to commodities typically produced in the South. The grain trade—the apparent cause of the legislation—was actually affected to little or no degree; Italy's exports were negligible even before 1887, and decreased still further thereafter, while imports, which appear dramatically smaller if we compare 1888 with the abnormal previous year, actually increased from a yearly average of 400,000 tons in 1880–86 to almost 700,000 in 1888–94. The commodities that did suffer most were wine, olive oil, liquorice and citrus fruit, whose previously upward export trends turned sharply downward. This was not due to price mechanisms, however, but to the predictable retaliations taken by the importing countries, whose boycotts and embargoes targeted southern products in particular. France—Italy's major trading partner, especially as regards southern farm commodities—responded to the protectionist measures with a tariff war that struck mainly at wine, oil and liquorice, while Russia imposed a 300 per cent tariff on Italian citrus fruits.

The losses in terms of outlets were not compensated by the tariffs' impact on prices. As far as grain was concerned, the tariffs, as we have seen, did not slow the inflow of foreign wheat but simply prevented a further fall in its price. While this had indeed a stimulating effect on capitalist farmers in Northern Italy, who were able to take advantage of protection and upgrade wheat production, for the *latifondisti*—who had held their own against American wheat, because of their low production costs—it spelt the loss of their main competitive advantage. In fact, the South's grain output plummeted.

The new policy thus created *de facto* protection for Northern Italy's farm commodities at the expense of the South's producers, peasants and *latifondisti* alike. Northern commodities began to saturate the domestic market, driving

out those of the South, while the reprisals taken by Italy's
trading partners were closing foreign outlets for the South's
specialized products. These effects might have been un-
intended, but they were perfectly predictable. The obvious step
for the *latifondisti* to take in their own interests would have
been simply to oppose the tariff. In this perspective their role
in enacting the 1887 legislation appears both illogical and self-
defeating.

Political alliances and the historic bloc

It is almost a commonplace belief that the protectionist
legislation of 1887 was a deal struck between Northern industrialists and Southern agrarians, which subsequently gave birth
to the so-called historic bloc. The agrarian party, composed of
Northern 'capitalists' and Southern 'feudalists' but oddly and
significantly headed by a Northern industrialist, Alessandro
Rossi, forced this volte-face on the traditionally free-trade
Parliament. There is no question as to the role played by the
representatives of Northern industry: understandably, they
wanted the government's protection for nascent industries and
their position was eventually justified by the policy's success.
However, the role played by the Southern components of the
agrarian party appears more ambiguous, considering that the
alliance was to wreak havoc on their enterprises and throughout the Southern agricultural economy. Were they aware of
those dangers? Giustino Fortunato suggested that, in their
shortsightedness, they were not: 'We southerners, seduced by
the mirage of a wheat tariff, allowed ourselves to be persuaded
by the exaggerated claims of the Po valley factories . . .'[8]

There is plenty of evidence, however, that not only were the
latifondisti aware, but that they opposed the tariff legislation as
long as they possibly could, ultimately surrendering only to the
logic (shortsighted indeed!) of political bargaining. Southern
deputies, almost all landowners themselves, had always been
free-traders, both because 'the fortunes of agriculture in
general and the South's in particular were tied to free trade'[9]
and because they did not want the government to intervene in

their affairs. They had already fought customs reform in 1878, worried by probable retaliation; in a country economically weak like Italy, argued Ascanio Branca, 'a tariff war would actually benefit only a few industrialists, who would levy a tax on the entire nation, and this would create purely artificial interests'.[10] In 1887 their position had been the same as it was to become in 1878. Towards the end of the year—when the treaty with France, denounced by Italy, was to expire on 31 December, and the Paris negotiations were deadlocked—the Association of Landowners and Farmers of the Provinces of Naples (of which Roberto Barracco had been a founder in 1866) called on the government to take 'Italian agricultural production into consideration . . . in the future trade treaties'. The resolution argued that 'the great annual variability of products [required] regular and convenient foreign outlets' and that a trade war would cause 'irreparable discouragement to the already shaky agricultural economy'.[11] No mention was made of prices.

There were voices among the Southern landowners in favour of protection, but they came almost exclusively from a compact group of Sicilian (absentee) landowners led by Camporeale. Their aggressive lobbying in 1885–87 did not, however, reflect the stand of *latifondisti* on the peninsula mainland. For example, of the thirty petitions in favour of a grain tariff addressed to the Chamber in 1885, not one came from Calabria; the only Calabrian landowner who spoke in favour of grain protection was Antonio Cefaly, a member of the opposition. *L'Agricoltura Meridionale,* the organ of the Association of Landowners and Farmers of the Provinces of Naples and a bastion of technologically 'progressive' *latifondismo* stuck to its guns: 'to weather the crisis, a remedy should be sought not in import tariffs but in a transformation of the system of cultivation . . .'[12] In fact, the conspicuous group of *latifondisti* in Parliament—the two Barraccos, Chimirri, Compagna, de Blasii, de Rudini, Farina, Fortunato, Giusso, Guarnieri, Maiorana Calatabiano, Piedimonte d'Alife, Pavoncelli and Quintieri—remained resolutely free-trade in their convictions. This fact did not escape Alessandro Rossi, who demagogically stressed at an Agrarian Defence rally held in Verona in 1887 that 'the feudalists [were] against import duties'.[13]

In a pamphlet published fifteen years later Napoleone Colajanni, patently irritated by the generalizations circulating with regard to the alliance of 1887, made it clear that the Southern parliamentary group, in which he included also the Sicilian barons, had not contributed at all to the swing towards protectionism. According to him,

> The whole great movement in favour of a protectionist reform of customs duties was exclusively northern: politicians, industrialists and chambers of commerce—organizations that in the *Mezzogiorno* had barely begun to show signs of life—promoted it in the North, and there was no initiative or contribution from the South.[14]

But, while it is true that the mainland *latifondisti* made no contribution to the enactment of protectionist legislation, they certainly put up no great opposition to it. When the tariff bill came to a vote in the Senate in April of 1887, and in the Chamber in June, most of the *latifondisti* lawmakers were absent. If not promotors of the movement, the Southern *latifondisti* did provide at least their passive support. Epicarmo Corbino's claim that 'the sacrifice of the South was not made deliberately, but almost unwittingly' credits the Southern representatives with great altruism. According to him, even 'when immediate and direct economic interests of a private or only regional nature were at stake, [their] decisions were usually dictated by the desire to safeguard the general interest of the Nation.'[15] But that altruism was clearly not there when, during the same period, the *latifondisti* staunchly opposed other measures introduced by the government under the same banner of the 'general interest of the nation' (which meant the disastrous financial situation and the difficulties encountered during the country's first exercises in imperialism) such as property tax equalization, railroad construction and war taxes.

The surrender of the *latifondisti* on the tariffs issue must be seen in the political–rhetorical context of the period, which made it difficult for the *latifondisti* to vote against the government. In the rhetoric of its proponents, protectionism was presented as the means to isolate the farmworkers movement: according to Alessandro Rossi, it would shield small landowners from Socialist influences; in the words of his secretary Egisto Rossi, it could even 'prevent a revolution that might drag the country into a social catastrophe'.[16] The government, they said, relied on the agrarians 'in view of the spread of socialism among the masses' and expected just a little sacrifice from them. In this context, though fairly indifferent to this issue (as farmworkers' organizations had as yet barely appeared in the South), and though embittered by the government's ploy, the traditionally Conservative *latifondisti* could hardly vote against the government in company with the far Left.

There were also global landed economic interests to be defended which demanded that the agrarians present in the Parliament a compact 'rural front'. In reality, the interests of landlords and tenants, absentee landlords and owner-operators, Northerners and Southerners, were far from homogeneous. Even among the Southern landowners the *latifondista*–entrepreneurs, like the Barraccos, or the Pavoncellis, were a minority. The issue at stake—tariffs, property tax equalization, the three-tenths war surtax on property and the revision of the railroad construction plan— found the so-called 'agrarian party' divided. The tariffs were opposed by the *latifondisti*, while they were advocated by some absentee Sicilian landowners and by the Northern agrarians whose heavily mortgaged properties could not bring profit below a certain price level.[17] Tax equalization would benefit Northern farmers at the expense of their Southern counterparts; repeal of the war tax would benefit all farmers; the revised railroad construction plan would hurt all regions south of Rome. The question of tariffs has been discussed already, but a few words need to be said about the other three issues.

Land tax equalization for the sake of fiscal justice had been the subject of parliamentary debates ever since Italian unity. The target was the tax privilege enjoyed by Southern land-owners, who, compared to their counterparts in other regions, paid less in property tax not only, and not so much, because the property registers of their regions were less accurate and less onerous, but above all because they possessed large quantities of unregistered ('usurped') land. The principle of fairly distributed taxation, dressed as it was in *Risorgimento* rhetoric, could hardly be refuted by anybody, but the Southern deputies argued, not without reason, that the tax burden as a whole weighed disproportionately on the South. Accordingly, they demanded as a precondition for equalization a lower property tax, and, more specifically, the repeal of the three-tenths war surtax. The latter faced stern opposition in Parliament on the basis that it would favour only the large landowners and bring little relief to agriculture in general, while considerably worsening the nation's already disastrous finances. Also the railroad issue was intertwined with fiscal rhetoric. In view of financial emergency, the government proposed to cut back and slow down its ambitious railroad construction plan. Such a retrenchment, however, would be discriminatory towards the South, whose railroad system, already inferior at Unification, was allocated only half the amount of public investment that had been given to the Northern railroads. The Southern landowners claimed that the planned revision would hurt the interests of export farming in general, and theirs in particular.[18]

All the issues were interconnected, and the *latifondisti* had to come to a compromise: to obtain tax relief, they had to form a united front with all the agrarians, thus to trade railroads for tariffs, and if they wanted the government's support, they would have to accept equalization. The governments of Depretis and Crispi played astutely on the agrarians' fears and on the divisions within the 'agrarian party'. In November 1885 the government submitted an omnibus law decree which linked tax relief to equalization. The trick worked: the equalization law was put through on 5 February 1886, with the landowners' vote. It created the precedent and the setting, with the railroad issue still pending and the threat of suspension of the war-tax repeal, for the final battle on grain tariff.

The tariff was introduced in an emergency bill by Finance Minister Magliani in April 1887. With the news of the massacre of Italian troops at Dogali still fresh, in the midst of a widely shared *spirito di rivincita* ('spirit of revenge') and general concern about public finances, the government had an easy job appealing demagogically to the landowners' spirit of sacrifice. The *latifondisti* found themselves caught in a political squeeze, between the government's budgetary needs, the Northern industrialists' claims of maximum protection even for the weakest industries, and some agrarians' demands for tariffs as a matter of justice for the 'agricultural industry' in a country where all other industries were protected. They opted for the unity of the agrarian party, making it possible to defeat the government's war-tax bill on a committee vote and obtaining the support of the Northerners on the railroad issue. Thus it was that in June 1887 the grain tariff was passed by a large majority in the Chamber.

As Antonio Gramsci noticed, Francesco Crispi's general policy was to strengthen Northern industrialists with the tariff war against France and protection against imports. In addition, the 'sovereign remedy' of grain protection did afford the Treasury an extra income of 365 million lire in one decade and it did allow Northern farmers to increase greatly their grain production—by 120 per cent in Piedmont, by 38 per cent in Lombardy and by 28 per cent in Emilia between 1885 and 1898. The South's grain output full by 42 per cent in the same period. For the South and the islands, the legislation spelled, as Gramsci wrote, 'a fearsome commercial crisis'.[19] It was indeed, in Stefano Jacini's bitter words, 'a plunder of the rural South by Italy's politicians'.

From the guarantist *latifondo* to the capitalist *latifondo*

The *latifondisti* were far from being the main victims of the protectionist policy. While it is true that some powerful *latifondisti* families, like the Mollos and the Ferrari d'Epaminondas, saw their fortunes wane, the more aggressive ones, like the Barraccos, the Berlingieris, or the Compagnas, set out to seek remedies. The new situation required new solutions.

The Barraccos' main problem was declining income. They were hardly in real financial straits, but by the end of the century liabilities on their properties had climbed to almost 2 million lire (roughly a third of their equity) and palaces and properties were run down. The old remedy—increasing output—was impracticable both because cheap new land was no longer available and because the market was saturated. There was nothing for it but to reduce, change, or transform production. Faithful to their modernizing mentality, the Barraccos opted for the structural transformation of the *latifondo*'s production and social organization. The changes they operated were essentially three: the scaling down of production, the upgrading of product quality and techniques and the modification of labour relations. To the extent that some changes in this direction had already been introduced in the pre-crisis years, the solution was not altogether new. In the 1880s and 1890s, however, the changes were carried out in an organized and global way that defined the character of the new *latifondo*.

Every single line of production was downsized. The first to be cut back was grain production, which was reduced by altering the same factor—planted acreage—that had been used to increase it in the past. The Barraccos sold no land—that would have been contrary to their gentleman–*latifondista* tradition—but they stopped cultivating marginal land, yielded in decades-old lawsuits over public lands, and reduced the number of *masserie* (farms). Resources released from grain production were not transferred to other sectors. The Barraccos continued the reorganization and downsizing of sheep rearing, sold some stocks *en bloc* and in 1898 owned only one of the five flocks they had owned in the past. The liquorice works in Neto, which had operated since 1812, was shut down in 1891, the Amantea works had closed some time before, so that at the end of the century only the San Pietro works were still operating with liquorice output down by half. In 1888 the Barraccos began to shut down their oil presses, too—the huge old works in Polligrone and the smaller ones in Trigani, Cupo, Cardinale and Lupia. By the end of the century the aggregate output of the remaining presses had fallen to about 30 per cent of the average for the 1870s or one-sixth of the figure for 1887, a bumper year.

Reduction of output proceeded hand in hand with further specialization and 'modernization'. More and more of the smaller acreage was planted with prime white wheat. The remaining *masserie* were equipped with Bodin and Bodin–Cantoni seeders, steel ploughs, Alen plough-harrows and steam threshers. The one flock left consisted solely of merino, Swiss and Rambouillet sheep. Those engaged in rearing cattle took pains with the industry's public image, showing prize stock at local and national fairs. Oil production, faced with market contraction and growing competition from seed and mineral oils, was upgraded as well: new Mure presses were installed and oil extraction from heated olives introduced, and products were shown at exhibitions. The liquorice works was equipped with mechanical rollers and tannin extractors, and greater attention was paid to product quality.

Lastly—and this was the real unspoken dimension of the whole process of modernization—the *latifondisti* transformed old labour arrangements, with repercussions the extent of which they themselves had not fully realized. Like most European landowners, in their response to the Great Depression, the Barraccos opted for labour efficiency.[20] For the sake of productivity and rational management they eliminated multi-use leases, thus depriving the workers of access to land. Crop specialization led to a gradual monetization of wages and the disappearance of remuneration in kind. The regular workforce, which had been decreasing since the 1870s, dropped by a further 27 per cent between 1890 and 1899; at the end of the century the workforce stood at less than half the number for the mid-century. Hiring was drastically reduced as well: 152 people hired in the 1880s, as against 311 in the 1850s. Three new aspects came to characterize relations with the remaining workers: monetization, the demise of the guarantee system and anonymity.

Not only nominal wages, but the actual payments became fully monetary. Employees were paid a flat cash wage with no supply of commodities—no more pork distribution at Carnival time, no more *ricotta* cheese for shepherds, no shoes or wool for domestic labour. Wage payment became a more formal process; advances against future earnings and aid in cash and commodities during the off-season were a thing of the past. Now a worker was paid only for and by the months he actually put in at a job, with an advance at hiring time and the 'balance' at the end of the month. Moreover, debt was no longer tolerated. Even if wages were higher than before (they were on the rise throughout Italy), a flat cash wage was all a man could expect.

The reorganization of land use had eliminated the workers' ability to produce subsistence and perpetuate their peasant status; the monetization of wages further reduced their expectations of satisfaction of their needs. But the death blow to the guarantee system came with the destruction of its keystone: job security.

During the first half-century of the *latifondo*'s existence very few labourers were ever dismissed; all told, only thirty-two, an average of six per decade. After 1860 the number soared to an average of seventy per decade, a more than tenfold increase. Moreover, while in the past three out of every four men fired eventually returned, dismissals were now definitive. The administrators no longer felt obliged to state the reasons for dismissal; but when they did, these were the same as in past—disobedience, drunkenness, brawling, bearing weapons without a permit, theft, or carelessness on the job. Thus, it was not the workers' behaviour that changed, but the management's exercise of greater control and discipline. Moreover, many workers were fired for reasons that had nothing to do with their jobs in the *latifondo*, while such a case had occurred only once in the previous half-century. It became hard for a man to get his job back after military service; twelve draftees lost theirs after 1870, as against only one before that date. Lastly, after 1880, the *latifondo* began laying off sick and injured workers who in earlier days would have simply been assigned less strenuous work.

In addition to breaking the tradition of job security, the *latifondo* also ceased to act as a mediator and provider of services. A worker could no longer go to the *latifondo*'s own lawyer, notary, or doctor, procure a gun permit, or buy medicine with the master contributing his customary 'third'.

The jobs on the *latifondo* were now characterized by an

unprecedented anonymity. A worker hired at a flat wage entered the Barracco's employ solely as a seller of working time; his whole social existence, formerly so tightly bound up with the *latifondo* structure, was now outside the sphere of labour relations. The new labour relationship was strictly individual; there was no longer any hope of getting one's children and/or relatives onto the payroll.[21] The kinship networks that had played so important a part in assuring peace on the *latifondo* began to break down; while in the years 1850–59, there were eighty-four 'family groups' of two or more relatives (father and sons, brothers and brothers-in-law), the number dwindled to seven in the 1880s, and to barely three in the last decade of the century. Gone were the lineages of cattle- and hog-drivers, *massari* ('husbandmen'), overseers, shepherds and agents, who for generations had handed down their jobs and their knowledge, as well as their loyalty. In consequence, the new *latifondo*, no longer able to rely on the traditional patriarchal sources of authority and control, had to increase surveillance. There was also greater anonymity; the Barraccos' place in their social territory changed, too, becoming an absence more than a presence; they ceased to attend the great fairs and no longer contributed to local charities.

The new *latifondo* took on a harsher, more controlled and threatening look that would become familiar to scholars and political observers at the turn of the century. Yet the transformations made by the Barraccos responded to criteria of economic rationality implemented in many parts of the continental South. From the Apulian plain to the hinterland of Naples and Crotone, the *latifondisti* were striving to modernize their large cereal- and stock-raising enterprises. The Barraccos, like the Pavoncellis and the Berlingieris, took actions rationally aimed at preserving their own fortunes and class privileges. From the standpoint of economic performance, their activism was crowned with success. The new management, which now employed college graduates in economics, was energetic and able; specialized products found outlets (admittedly limited) in the domestic market; and technical progress continued. In making these transformations, however, the *latifondisti* unwittingly set in motion a process of capitalist transformation of the *latifondo* system itself, and of its social territory, engendering contradictions in the political and social sphere that were to prove insurmountable and led to the system's demise.

The *latifondo* had become vulnerable. The new anonymous relationship with the workers was antagonistic and, given the right occasion, could become explosive. After all traditional contracts and partnerships and all the elements of the guarantee system had been swept away, the only bond between the masters and the mass of employees became the impersonal one between them as buyers and sellers of working time. Since there was now nothing else to tie a worker to the *latifondo* and the number of emigrants was increasing, the owners encountered growing difficulty in recruiting hands. The transformations further increased the market dependence of both the enterprise and its workers. As the enterprise came to operate on a strictly monetary basis, it depended ever more on the availability of outlets for its products and it also had to take greater account of market prices. And since the workers' subsistence now depended solely on the buying power of their wages, they were emboldened to voice protest and to fight for better pay. Protests against the mill tax (the notorious 'hunger tax') were directed not, as one might have expected, against government, but against the Barraccos and their gristmills, as the old *minatico* of rye 'to be ground at the master's expense' was replaced by a cash wage that had to cover both grain purchases and the tax payable at the mill.[22]

Thus it was that the *latifondismo* waned at the end of the century amid 'warnings, and portents and evils imminent': phylloxera, which destroyed the vineyards, oil flies, which decimated the olive groves, the earthquake of 1894, dramatically increased emigration, and the short-lived but intense class struggles of 1898.[23] During most of the nineteenth century, *latifondismo* had constituted a true social and economic system in which 'each element [was] inseparable from all the others and from the mechanism governing their interaction, which preserved and constantly reproduced the overall arrangement according to what might be called its own laws'.[24] Its demise was not a direct result of the Great Depression: the system declined because the crisis, and the subsequent commercial policy followed by Italy, made it harder to market the *latifondo*'s products and thus spurred the owners into an economic dynamism that completed the process of capitalist transformation touched off by the legal reforms of the French decade. In its eighty years of existence *latifondismo* had successfully blended the traditional and the modern, in its own autonomous rationality. When it cast the modernist lot, it dug its own grave. *Latifondismo* expired without heirs. Its successor was the capitalist *latifondo* that never possessed or attempted to develop the cohesive mechanisms of a true and proper socio-economic system.

NOTES

1. For further information on *latifondismo* see M. Petrusewicz, *Latifundium: Moral Economy and Material Life in a European Periphery* (Michigan, 1996), an in-depth study of the economic, social and moral functioning of the largest nineteenth-century Calabrian *latifondo*, based on the exceptionally rich and complete private archive of the Barracco family.

   The publication of this book in Italian in 1989 sparked a lively controversy concerning the character and the rationality of the *latifondo* and the historical role played by *latifondismo*. See in particular the review by Adrian Lyttelton and the exchange it generated on the pages of the *Times Literary Supplement* between Giancarlo de Vivo, John Davis, Piero Bevilacqua, Adrian Lyttelton and Marta Petrusewicz (4 October, 8, 29 November, 6, 27 December 1991; 31 January, 14 February, 6 March 1992). Most recently Giovanni Montroni returned to the debate in his *Gli uomini del re: La nobiltà napoletana nell'Ottocento* (Rome, 1996). The present chapter cannot respond to all the criticisms, but it does restate the basic argument and attempts to clarify the mechanisms by which Southern agricultural production was excluded from the market—an issue raised by Professor Lyttelton.

2. The main inspiring references in my conceptualization of *latifondismo* and its specific rationality are: A.V. Chayanov, *The Theory of Peasant Economy* (Illinois, 1966) and his 'The Socio-Economic Nature of the Peasant Farm Economy', in P.A. Sorokin, C.C. Zimmerman and C.J. Galpin, eds, *A Systematic Source Book in Rural Sociology* (Minneapolis, 1931); W. Kula, *An Economic Theory of the Feudal System* trans. L. Garner (London, 1976); K. Polanyi, *The Great Transformation: The Political and Economic Origins of Our Time* (Boston, 1968); and E.P. Thompson, 'The Moral Economy of the English Crowd in the 18th Century', *Past and Present*, 50 (1971).

3. We are here concerned with the specialized products of the *latifondo*, which in its 'two-track' economy were destined for sale in distant

markets, but the decline also involved the 'poorer' commodities produced for the local markets.

4. The most important factors that made the *latifondo* economy so profitable were the following: (i) low cost of land which was acquired at a low price, inherited, or 'usurped', and not subject to calculations of comparative advantage; (ii) cheap labour available in practically 'unlimited supply'; (iii) wages computed in pecuniary terms but in reality largely paid in goods and services that never entered the cash economy; (iv) estates mostly unencumbered by mortgages, which vice versa weighed heavily on land revenues in Northern Italy.

5. W. Kula has described similar mechanisms of reaction among seventeenth-century Polish nobility in his masterful *An Economic Theory of the Feudal System*. A. Hirschman, in *Passions and Interests* (Princeton, 1977), uses a similar argument in respect of the political reaction of the aristocrats (or 'gatekeepers').

6. J.A. Davis, *Merchants, Monopolists, and Contractors* (New York, 1981).

7. This increase actually did not occur. Per capita grain consumption in Italy was 0·5 litres a day in 1870–74 and dropped to 0·27 litres in 1897–8. Although the 1897–8 figure is statistically not significant, as this was a year of terrible dearth, there seems to be no question that popular consumption failed to increase over this period.

8. G. Fortunato, *Il Mezzogiorno e lo stato italiano*, 1 (Bari, 1911), 277.

9. G. Carocci, *Agostino Depretis e la politica interna italiana dal 1876 al 1887* (Turin, 1956), 442. While Carocci acknowledges that over this whole period protectionist pressure encountered substantial opposition from Southern and agrarian interests, he maintains that during Depretis's last government 'wide sectors of the southern bourgeoisie were being converted to protectionism' (442). In this, his otherwise precise and reliable discussion is rather vague. He makes no distinction between those Southern parliamentarians who spoke for the new bourgeoisie of midscale landowners and professionals and those who represented the great *latifondisti*, just as he does not distinguish between Sicilians and mainlanders.

10. A speech in the Chamber of Deputies on 17 June 1878. Quoted by G. Carocci, *Agostino Depretis*, 442n.

11. The text of the petition was published in *L'Agricoltura Meriodionale*, 1 January 1888, 4–5.

12. R. Arcuri, 'Aiutiamo l'agricoltura' *L'Agricoltura Meridionale* (January 1885), 122.

13. As reported by N. Colajanni, *L'Agricoltura veronese* (1887), 4.

14. As reported by N. Colajanni, *Per l'economia nazionale e pel dazio sul grano* (Rome, 1901), 24–7.

15. *Annali dell'economia italiana*, 3 (Citta di Castello, 1993), 23.

16. E. Rossi, *Stati Uniti e concorrenza americana* (Florence, 1884), 56ff.

17. Mortgage debt encumbered 34 per cent of land revenues in Piedmont and 21 per cent in Lombardy, but only 14 per cent in the Neapolitan provinces and 10 per cent in Sicily. See L. Musella, *Proprieta e politica agraria in Italia* (Naples, 1984), 16.

18. This is the data cited in Parliament by Rocco de Zerbi, a fierce opponent of the bill:

	Authorized by law	Railroad Expenses Appropriated in the budget	Spent or committed
North of Rome	408,875,000	203,047,227	540,932,007
South of Rome	578,674,000	158,562,254	247,822,548

19. In his gloss on an article by S. Valitutti, Gramsci noted that 'agrarian protectionism benefited the North more than the South, because it protected grain, of which the North was a great producer (relatively more than the South)', *Quaderni dal carcere*, ed. V. Gerratana, 3 (Turin, 1975), 2018 (Quaderno 19); ibid., 1804–05 (Quaderno 15).

20. 'The main incentive to change', writes E. Hobsbawm, 'came from the well-known tendency of profit-margin to decline in the Great Depression . . . Whether pressure from competition or from labour was more important in turning employers' thoughts towards labour efficiency is uncertain' *Labouring Men* (New York, 1967), 421.

21. A. Chayanov emphasized how important it was for peasant families, who frequently found themselves with temporary surpluses of labour, to satisfy the need to employ these extra members: 'since the subjective significance of its satisfaction is valued higher than the burden of labour necessary for such satisfaction, the peasant family will work for a smaller remuneration that would be definitely unprofitable in a capitalist economy' ('The Socio-Economic Nature of the Peasant Farm Economy').

22. In 1880, women were demanding 1.25 lire a day to work in the Barraccos' spinning mills in the Sila, though the pay in Cosenza was only 85 centimes, because the wages paid in the Sila had to cover everything from food to lodging.

23. One hundred and five people emigrated from the province of Catanzaro in 1876, 142 in 1880, 1,581 in 1885, 5,092 in 1888, 8,733 in 1893, and 10,420 in 1900: an increase of 10,000 per cent in twenty years! Already in 1883 Leopoldo Franchetti had denounced the spoliation of the peasantry of which the Italian government, together with all the political parties, including the far Left, was both author and accomplice.

24. M. Rossi Doria, 'Strutture e problemi dell'agricoltura meridionale', *Riforma agraria e azione meridionalista* (Bologna, 1956), 9.

3

Local Power in Southern Italy

Paolo Pezzino

This chapter offers a brief overview of the formation of a
critical tradition concerning the exercise of local power in the
South through an analysis of the work of several of the classic
meridionalisti. It then discusses the arguments advanced by
'historical revisionism' which has recently focused on the
themes of the Italian *Mezzogiorno*. Finally, it indicates the weak
points of the new research and suggests the criteria necessary
to establish an approach that can carefully evaluate which
elements of the great tradition of *meridionalismo* may still be
considered valid.

'In constitutional states such as Italy, which draw their
strength and support from the middle class, the foundation of
the entire mechanism of government resides in local influence,'
wrote Leopoldo Franchetti in his study of Sicily in 1876.

> 'The Ministry governs by means of the majority of deputies of
> the Chamber, and the election of the latter depends to a large
> extent on persons who for sundry reasons may influence the
> votes of electors in every electoral college . . . Since the wants
> and wishes articulated by these influential figures determine the
> choice of one deputy as opposed to another, they are neces-
> sarily considered to be the same as the wants and wishes of the
> country . . . Thus the authority of influential persons in each
> area, whatever the origin and cause of this influence, is
> recognized, sanctioned and utilized by the Government; hence,
> the persons thus identified also constitute the dominant class in
> politics and in administration. It follows that if on the one hand

the direct intervention of the dominant class in local administration is, up to a certain point, subject to Government control
by virtue of the laws in force, on the other hand, there can be
no appeal against intervention deriving from the influence of
that very class on the direction of the Government itself.[1]

Franchetti provided an exemplary synthesis of the organic-
functionalist concept of representation typical of the Liberal
ruling class in the period immediately following Unification; he
also illustrated the problem of local power in the South. In
addition, Franchetti pointed out that in Sicily (but his
observations could be extended beyond the island itself) 'the
wealthy class numbers very few members, and within it
influence and authority are the exclusive monopoly of a very
few'.[2] Sicily thus lacked any mediating, authority between
central government and the localities an authority normally
exercised by the solid bourgeois, landowning class, to whom
this power would be awarded by a property-based suffrage.
The reasons behind this, Franchetti argued, lay in such factors
as the extremely small numbers of the population belonging to
the middle class, the character of the society (in many respects
still feudal) and a conception of the law in which the 'material
force' of a handful of influential individuals was still the
decisive element in imposing the will and interests of these
individuals themselves. This contrasted with what Franchetti
saw as the true nature of the middle class, for, as Franchetti
wrote, 'it is a hallmark of the middle class that each one of the
individuals making up the class does not have the capacity to
force observance of his own interests by coercion'.[3] For all
these reasons, then, the application of an institutional system
founded on a considerable extension of the autonomy and
prerogatives of local administration had caused serious harm,
given that, as Sonnino added, 'through our institutions . . . we
provided the oppressor class with a better means to cloak in
legal forms the *de facto* oppression that already obtained'.[4]

These themes were by no means new ones in Italy, as the
issue of the limits of the system of local autonomy had arisen
in the very early years of the new state. In the *Mezzogiorno*,
however, these questions took on a particular tone, because the
quality of Southern society did not appear to be reconcilable

with an extension of Liberal institutions: political struggle was petty and mean-minded, and provided a battleground for factions and hangers-on, while the family unit appeared to be the only truly solid social bond among the people. 'The community that remains most vigorous among individuals of such a nature is . . . the family community', wrote Turiello, 'and thence it follows that beyond the confines of the family, hardly any other moral bonds are to be found'. The 'only tie that appears to find a natural and efficacious base there [i.e. in the South], above and beyond the family',[5] was an allegiance based on hangers-on seeking favours. Thus the mainland *Mezzogiorno* was seen as anchored to a pre-political structuring of social relations, founded on primary bonds and on the intrinsic weakness of institutional authorities, at both state and local level.

As a consequence the decentralizing Liberals were reproached for adopting an abstract doctrinaire outlook by appealing to the glorious Italy of the *comuni* without taking into account the real social situation in the Southern countryside. This, it was held, was characterized by an absentee but avaricious bourgeoisie and an impoverished and ignorant populace. Turiello realized that in the *Mezzogiorno*, instead of a hegemony of the landowners, which was indispensable for the functioning of a property-based representational system, the prevailing situation was one of fierce hatred between landowners and peasants, fuelled by the overthrow of feudalism when the bourgeoisie took over the role of overlord hitherto played by and maintained the harsh contractual terms that had been imposed upon the peasants. Hence the call for a just and proper administration, in contrast to the 'parliamentarianism' that opponents of Depretis' transformism criticized as weak, unprincipled and open to bias and the influence of favouritism. The only apparent alternative for the South was innovative and impartial action (shielded from the bias induced by political choices) on the part of the state's administrative institutions relying on their capacity to impose some sort of modernization on the South's social structure from above.

It is no coincidence that the rejection of the influence in

Southern Italy of a grasping and absentee middle class, ignorant and obtuse, shaped by family structure and clientage, and far removed from the hegemonic models of agrarians in Lombardy or Tuscan landowners was first voiced during the period of 'parliamentary revolution' after 1876, when the Left ousted the Historic Right: a watershed in the political history of the Kingdom. Nor is it a coincidence that the charges were brought first and foremost by representatives and theoreticians of the Historic Right, who were anchored to a rigidly élitist conception of the state and to an ethical–pedagogical perception of the role of a ruling class. The forces of the Right were hostile to the demand for expansion of the area of power that came from the Left, and opposed both the demand for the extension of suffrage and the call for administrative decentralization—themes dear to the Left. The Right on the contrary stressed the low quality of political mediation in the South, the inadequacy of the landowners' hegemony and the lack of administrative justice.

One result of this were proposals for an expansion of suffrage in a conservative sense, with the aim of guaranteeing a property-owning hegemony. These proposals sought to identify the modern political means for the construction of an organic framework that would embody a resolution of the conflict (one need only think of the favourable attitude towards universal suffrage—albeit tempered by compensatory mechanisms—evidenced by Jacini and Sonnino,[6] or the 'conservative decentralization' advocated by di Rudini).[7] But within Liberal *meridionalismo* a critique of parliamentarianism prevailed. This led to the call for restrictions on the autonomy of local action and political struggle in favour of a more incisive presence of the state that would regulate the involvement of local interests. Turiello, reaffirming the position of Sonnino, declared:

> In truth our much-vaunted glorious position of possessing the greatest local autonomy in Europe today can be said to amount to our having granted the greatest authority and jurisdictional power to a few persons elected by a single class, while only allowing the individual Italian a minimum level of real freedom.[8]

In assessing the analyses of *meridionalismo*, whether moderate or reformist, recent historiography has shown increasing signs of disagreement with the picture of the South that emerges, judging it to be both unilateral and static. Exponents of *meridionalismo* are accused of having portrayed the South as a separate area, in which the various stages and events of national history appear to be of very little significance, either as regards economic development or the more specific political–institutional questions. The ceaseless insistence upon the parasitic and favour-seeking characteristics of the bourgeoisie, it is claimed, ignored the development of more complex forms of political organization that expressed a variety of social interests. These began to come to the fore from the 1880s onwards, in a process parallel to that which was observed, and more extensively studied, in the central northern region of the country. It should also be noted that the forms of local power themselves underwent progressive change after Unification, in conjunction with the evolution of legislation and the pressure of organized social forces, as the South too experienced a growth in functions assigned to city government.

From the point of view of this new historiographical tendency, the study of changes in the institutional and political setup of local power cannot but lead to a reappraisal of the character of the Southern local élites, which were previously either classed together without distinction by *meridionalismo* under the generic definition of *piccola borghesia* (petty bourgeoisie), or else frozen in totalitarian visions such as that of the 'agrarian bloc' theorized by Gramsci. These static and immobile élites appeared to dominate the local scene, clinging to the base defence of their own privileges, and confined within a stifling and blinkered vision. They faced a state that was variously depicted as impotent, centralizing, corrupt, bureaucratic, and that always emerged as the losing party in any attempt to impose order on the disarray of the South.

Recent historiography has stressed, however, that the conception outlined above of the uniform predominance of the landowning classes does not in fact correspond to reality: hand in hand with urban development and state intervention new classes emerged as traditional hegemonies became obsolete. Even agriculture experienced new forms of production and a new social equilibrium among those who depended on it for their subsistence.

Such reassessments are in many respects justified by the stale repetitiveness of the historiography of the *Mezzogiorno* in the 1960s and 1970s which, with only a few exceptions, uncritically reiterated the judgement passed by exponents of *meridionalismo*. Having acknowledged, however, that 'historical revisionism' breathes an invigorating spirit of renewal into this field of study, its theses require detailed scrutiny and raise a number of doubts in my mind: there is a risk of allowing oneself to be lured into a simple-minded inversion of the judgement of backwardness and immobilism that has enjoyed overwhelming predominance so far within the historiography. There may even be the danger that revision, could ultimately deny the existence of a *questione meridionale*—a 'Southern question. In other words, rather than elaborating a definition of the North–South dualism by means of modern techniques and extensive examination in order to reconstruct an overall picture (that cannot but form a complex chiaroscuro), an uncompromising stance may be adopted. This stance would deny the very existence of dualistic analysis, restricting discussion to a polemic against *meridionalismo* that now appears sterile and outdated.

Before an understanding of the roles, size and true modernizing inclinations of the bourgeois élite can be reached, much more research is required. According to the new historians of the *Mezzogiorno*, it was a modern and progressive group, linked to urban government. Villani states that its origins are to be found in the late eighteenth century, in 'a particular type of agrarian bourgeoisie' composed of 'tenants, usurers, cattle-breeders, administrators of feudal estates, overlords of baronial land and estates, mayors and officials of the local administration, medium and small-size traders'.[9] But far too little is known as yet for an opinion to be passed on whether the polemics surrounding the lack of civic virtues, in this new ruling class, as displayed in the squandering of local finances and the mismanagement of the fiscal system (polemics which extended from the end of the eighteenth century uninterrupted until the post-Unification period), arose purely from political prejudice. Rather than such outright judgements, what is required is a study of the rise of this new social stratum and its position in the processes of modernization that characterized the nineteenth century and involved not only the economic sphere, but political and administrative affairs as well. This will enable the complex processes of implementation of the institutional reforms enacted during the last century to be more readily situated within the various social contexts of the *Mezzogiorno*. This is the theme on which I propose to dwell.

It cannot be denied that from the second half of the eighteenth century onwards the local community was the classic launch pad for the Southern bourgeoisie's rise to political power, and as a result the members of this class found themselves in conflict with the feudal nobility. The importance of the local level was further strengthened during the period of the Restoration, with the establishment of new bodies, such as the elected town council, the *comune* (replacing the feudal *università*), and the district and provincial councils. The policy of reform encountered contradictory responses in the sharply divergent local situations throughout the Kingdom: nevertheless this hierarchical modernization left a permanent mark on the social and political life of the early nineteenth-century *Mezzogiorno*. In effect it represented the attempt to subject 'civil administration' . . . the basis of public prosperity . . . to uniform rules throughout all our dominions' (Royal decree, 11 October 1817). Indeed the administrative order introduced by the law of 12 December 1816 set up a structure fashioned after the French model, dividing the territory into provinces, each of which was governed by an *intendente* endowed with broad powers of control and management. A uniform administration was thereby created, with a hierarchical structure, and entrusted with the task of firm control and supervision of the local authorities. These local bodies were administered by personnel nominated by the state authorities according to complex procedures based on lists of eligible persons. The lists included all proprietors having land above a certain annual rental value, a value determined by law and varying according to the size of the *comune*. The *comuni* were entrusted with tasks that were rigidly fixed by law (above all in fiscal affairs, town and rural police forces, hygiene, services, public works) and every deliberation of the *comune* was subject to approval by the *intendente*.

Despite this high level of centralization, the local élites did achieve a considerable degree of autonomy from the centre. Evidence shows that when these élites felt that their overall position was being eroded, then the considerable divergence of interest existing within their ranks receded into the background, allowing them to unite in order to offer maximum resistance to central government attempts at regulation and control. Frequently this resistance was a consequence of the autonomy experienced under the former regime, and a result of the presence of a sizeable urban aristocracy that derived confirmation of its status from the public offices held by its members within the local community. But even when the numbers of bourgeois were greater this did not lead to fractures in the fabric of the élite upon which the monarchy could have capitalized by attempting to supplant the nobility with a proprietorial middle class. Instead the bourgeois class appears to have forged an alliance with the nobility around the issue of the defence of local autonomy. A process was set in motion whereby nobility and bourgeoisie began to draw closer together. After 1815 nobles and bourgeois were prepared despite some episodes of conflict between them, to work together in exercising their old power on the bases established by the administrative reforms.

The contradiction inherent in the Bourbon reforms could not be clearer: the centralized structure of the new state ran into the resistance of local élites, and also paid the penalty for the ineffectual and half-hearted reforming intentions of the central power itself. The *intendente*, a pivotal figure of the whole system, was often unable to establish links with the nerve centre of the state that would have enabled a viable system to be formed. On the contrary, the *intendente* frequently headed unwieldy structures bedevilled by chronic shortages of means and staff, and consequently suffered all the inconveniences of the continual breakdowns in communication between the core and the peripheral structure of the administration, and between the latter and local society. It was only the *intendente*'s ability to resolve conflicts by informal means, together with the use of broad deviations from the law and from approved norms, that allowed him to assure the working of the system—at least to a minimum extent. In this manner the logic of mediation won out over the concept of control and supervision of local élites.

What could therefore be defined as 'functional' non-observance of the norms did mean, however, that in calmer periods, a certain administrative normality could be guaranteed, while in moments of political or social crisis a normative and institutional void existed, which was filled by the hegemonic capacity of local élites. Even though these élites were able to react to and influence the process of modernization, they themselves were considerably influenced by the Bourbon reforms. It was not so much the ideology or social composition of the élites that changed, but the imposition of limits on local power. Administrative law established a series of spheres in which local level intervention was applicable (fiscal affairs, health care, etc.), which, when compared to the undifferentiated autonomy under the former regime, actually represented a delimitation of local fields of action. The life and affairs of the *comune* were now run on new bases, and slowly but surely participation in local government began to represent not only a confirmation of intrinsic status, but also a source of new economic and 'political' opportunities, a means to revive old hegemonies and to boost the processes of elevation in social status. The *comune* was thus transformed into an instrument of power and gain for ever broader social groups. From the excise duties levied by town customs tolls to the increasing availability of jobs and appointments, new bargaining prospects were unfolding for the local élites, who increasingly modelled themselves on the forms typical of a local ruling class, in which status and prestige derived from the authority and influence they exerted over public affairs, rather than merely being the consequence of membership of a given social order. This was a process that can be defined in terms of social change, yet it is one which, in my view, does not evince the dynamic expansive character usually attributed to modernization. The contradictory features of this process were to come starkly to the fore after Unification: the new Liberal regime launched a quest for a middle class that could provide the backbone of its constitutional construct, only to find élites ready to carry out the new functions ascribed to them without having passed through any process of in-depth renewal.

Several essential components of this vicious circle can be distinguished here: first, the formation of a local power capable of eluding central control and resolutely held together by the ramifications of kinship, patronage and clientage that united local élites; second, the obstacles that state power was unable to overcome its endeavour to impose state norms and to discipline society within a local context, which did not share the state's ultimate goal of nation-building, and third, the involvement of representatives of the new institutions in the faction-ridden aspects of political struggle.

In this vicious circle there was an important connection, namely that between a lack of collective action and the tendency for social relations to cluster around interpersonal, family or kinship relations. These are precisely the focus of the study carried out by the American anthropologist Banfield.[10] His thesis concerning 'amoral familism' has been much criticized, but in my view Banfield did identify a crucial theme, worthy of greater attention than it has so far received. It can hardly be doubted that familism and factionism exerted profound influence on the mechanisms governing the form-ation of the state apparatus in the contemporary *Mezzogiorno* (beginning with the process of definite overthrow of feudalism in the early nineteenth century). By the same token, it influenced relations between the state and local ruling classes, who were to be both the protagonists and subjects of statism. This was the origin of an intolerable autonomy for the national state, namely the autonomy of Southern local élites, intent on perpetuating their own hegemony even in a period of profound institutional renewal.

This brings us back to the classic theme of the inadequacy of the bourgeois classes and their attitudes. Admittedly, as

Romanelli has recently argued, 'a variety of meanings cohabit within the 'bourgeois universe', but it cannot be doubted that:

> the greater structural fragility of Italy's southern provinces accentuates the dramatic nature of this amalgam . . . and carries its theoretical indeterminacy to the extreme. The study of a peripheral area of extreme instability thus suggests the need to concentrate on the relationships between the various components of modernization (economic, cultural and institutional), measurement of their internal hierarchies and theoretical evaluation).[11]

The theme of familism was very much to the fore in the uncompromising writings of the *meridionalisti* mentioned at the beginning of this chapter. This was the characteristic of the Southern peoples that Turiello defined as *sciolto*:

> Furthermore the common Italian characteristic as it appears in Neapolitan is almost closer to its origins than in other Italians; it is less rounded at the edges by the long-standing habit of civil coexistence, in the political and administrative consortia of medieval and modern times . . . The constitutions of Frederick II, which created the oldest inorganic and anti-feudal state to be established in Europe, for centuries left these individuals more unattached and freer from orders, *comuni*, and class bonds than perhaps in any other region.[12]

The description of this *scioltezza* does to some extent pander to what the editor of the most recent edition of Turiello's work, Piero Bevilacqua, defined as arguments of 'a subculture still operating today in common-place attitudes';[13] yet there is an important intuition of a link between the existence of a familistic subculture and the absence of associative traditions (traditions termed by Turiello 'social bonds'), the weakness of intermediate structures between the individual with his network of primary relations and the state. The *comune* could not possibly become an intermediate body capable, on its own, of filling this gap: on the contrary it was itself adversely affected by the *scioltezza* that was widespread in society, since at the administrative level this engendered the predominance of local clientage networks. In other words, in

Southern Italy the autonomy of the *comuni* did not appear to be governed by that network of 'corporations, non-profit-making bodies, associations and organs representing interests'[14] that elsewhere formed the fabric of communal autonomy, or indeed represented the latter's very essence, as illustrated for instance in the thought of the Moderate Tuscans who favoured decentralization.

This is an argument that might initially invite contradiction in the emphasis of the conservative aspects of the organic theories of the early *meridionalisti*, but I believe that if a correct account is to be given of the uncertain outcome of moderniz-ation processes in the *Mezzogiorno*, it is essential to take note of the weakness of what Turiello defined as the 'organic institutions of civilized peoples'.[15] Turiello was referring here to the process through which family bonds gradually give way to bonds of civil coexistence in a process of the institu-tionalization of social relations. The bonds of clientage and factionalism are of course not the exclusive property of Southern Italy, but in this context these are the relations that appear to have been absolutely predominant, to the extent of characterizing the entire gamut of political life and the com-plex spectrum of social relations. In the South one is thus faced with the persistence of the 'natural community' of the family (as the church has always conceived it). This 'com-munity' recycled itself without mediation into political circles and expanded into new spheres of activity as these arose within the new forms assumed by the institutions, whether it was a case of the administrative reforms of the early nineteenth century or those of the Liberal state.

Thus the reason why the modernizing and centralizing impulses of the Liberal state was so short-lived, and why this process was so much more uncertain and ambiguous when viewed from the local perspective can be readily understood. Very soon a process of co-optation of local élites set in, privileging the various accommodations by means of which a balance between the state and the élites could be reached, even though it must be stressed that the new equilibriums estab-lished were not merely repetitions of those of the past. Therefore, when studying the *Mezzogiorno* and the Italian situation, the model of relations between the periphery and the core which emerges can be seen to be founded neither on processes of the diffusion and homogenization of modernizing impulses radiating out from the centre, nor on relations of exploitation ('internal colonialism'). Rather, the predominant system was a complex system of mediations during the course of which the periphery—if we elect to continue using this term—did not restrict itself to resisting the core, but in fact influenced it, manipulated its norms, set up privileged relations with its peripheral agents, and exercised sway not only over the final outcomes, but also over the very approach to the process of modernization at the national level.

The Right's grand design for centralization, which has been so fiercely criticized by that historiography which favoured an expansion of local autonomy, remained, in fact, largely, ineffectual. The design proved unable to evolve into a cohesive political choice, and was compelled to entrust its fortunes to peripheral officials who were then left without 'cover'; thus it did not succeed in deploying its forces coherently, and remained more of a temporary choice than a determined show of force. This weakness within the government derived from a multiplicity of causes: lack of means, political isolation, insufficient social hegemony of those ruling classes that were manifesting support for the government, constant quarrels and skirmishes at the local level.

In the *Mezzogiorno* even those officials who had been inspired by the system of the self-government found them-selves compelled to observe that the *comune* was still far from being 'the initiator and regulator of a way of life, the representative of ancient glory, the precursor of future progress',[16] as Falconcini briefly prefect of Agrigento, wrote of the municipalities of Central and Northern Italy. In the South

> every small town is tyrannically ruled by the warlord that dominates it . . . The mayor was in almost all respects the despot of the *comune*, and his closest supporters fulfilled the role of sovereigns; the clashes between the most powerful families were grounded in the desire to be awarded municipal honours, and the civic magistrature was counted most naturally as the perfect means to dominate the town.[17]

This was one of the first of a series of exposées of the inadequate social structures of the Southern *comuni*. In the South there appeared to exist no intermediate level of mediation between the state and the primary structures of society (family and kinship relations), nor was there any trace of the intricate network of bodies, associations, and organized interests that could stand as a bulwark against both familial social relations and state despotism.

The problem was compounded by the weak social hegemony of the dominant classes in the South, which was probably due to the fact that in the eyes of the general public of the region very little sense of legitimacy attached to possession of land, since land ownership in the nineteenth century was still linked to an idea of violence, usurpation and illegality inflicted on the population. This feature was in its turn exacerbated by the general scarcity of resources and the growing imbalance between resources and the population as the people struggled to survive on what was available. This grim situation continued until the end of the century, and prevented the economic élite from founding and consolidating a system of relatively autonomous social authority, thereby rendering the ruling class weak and dependent on legitimation from outside the local area, that is from the central political power.

Beyond the bonds of kinship groups there were few structures (either associative or institutional) that could foster and channel social consensus towards the institutional system. The function of this consensus should have been to assure that civil society maintained proper respect for the norms and rules that lay at its foundation and were entrusted with the task of supporting it. But the lack of intermediate bodies, and the weakness of the state institutions themselves, led these regions into a precocious engagement in politics. The results, however, proved to be detrimental: the local élites hastened to occupy the new terrain opened up in the changed political arena without really sharing the goals of the new system.

This led to a permanent wariness on the part of the institutions towards civil society and towards its rules and customs. The state, in turn, did not have the capacity to establish a legitimizing institutional procedure, which would have been regarded by the local society and its ruling classes as an alternative to the clientage-based, factional, regimes. An alternative of this kind, forcibly imposed though it might have seemed in origin, could in the long run have achieved success. But in fact the ultimate outcome of this course of affairs was that the *Mezzogiorno* saw the rise of a powerful and headstrong 'dependence élite',[18] which succeeded in influencing the evolution of the process of political and social modernization over the last two centuries by playing the weakness of the state against its own persistent autonomy. The usurpation of public commodities (from water to publicly owned land, from contracts for control of excise duties to control of law enforcement and illicit activities such as rustling) reinforced the local élites in the first half of the nineteenth century, and developed alongside control over land ownership, gradually turning into a veritable process of legalization of the privileges of the emergent bourgeoisie. This process was recognized by contemporary institutional sources and viewed as having negative connotations, following an interpretative approach that saw it as signalling the emergence of a clientage-based system and of interests that could not be considered legitimate. The charge of 'factionalism' was levelled by these sources against both the two 'political' sides into which almost all small towns are divided, as each side constantly strove to drum up support and provide guarantees for private interests, licit or illicit, at the expense of the collectivity. It cannot be doubted that this negative characterization of the local political struggle also derived from the severe judgment passed on the bourgeoisie, deemed unsuitable for the task of running the complex mechanisms of regulation and control of the Liberal state (even if the same observations could also be applied to administration at the time of the Bourbon monarchy).

Historians should therefore enquire as to why an entire generation of politicians and officials should have moved within the short space of but a few years from an attitude that was generally favourable to administrative decentralization, albeit of a conservative type, to one of support for states of siege and periodic military campaigns. This is a question that reverts to the dramatic aspects of nation-building in Italy, and testifies to the lack of a deep-seated collective ethos in the social fabric, the absence of 'that reciprocal trust which lies at the base of all morally just civic life', to use the felicitous phrase of Peruzzi (one of the most influential figures of the Right).[19] Only with this trust can rulers implement choices that harm the interests of many of their subjects. There emerges a clear picture of the lack of such a trust between rulers and a middle class called upon to champion both the proposals of the Liberal centralizers and those of the democratic decentralizers. This was the obstacle against which policies directed towards the *Mezzogiorno* foundered, whether they were intended in one direction or the other.

Moreover, these same limitations have persisted up to the present day: nowadays all commentators consider renewal of the Southern political class, which has been supported by the extension of public intervention, as an essential condition for the rebirth of the *Mezzogiorno*—a rebirth that must be expressed first and foremost not so much in economic terms but above all in those of civic virtue.

NOTES

1. L. Franchetti and S. Sonnino, *La Sicilia I. Condizioni politiche e amministrative della Sicilia* (Florence, 1925) 269–71.
2. Ibid., 271.
3. Ibid., 87.
4. L. Franchetti and S. Sonnino, *La Sicilia II. I contadini in Sicilia*, 180.
5. P. Turiello, *Governo e governati in Italia*, ed., P. Bevilacqua (Turin, 1980), 59–60.
6. R. Romanelli, 'Alla ricerca di un corpo elettorale. La riforma del 1882 in Italia e il problema dell'allargamento del suffragio', *Il comando impossible. Stato e società nell'Italia liberale* (Bologna, 1988).
7. A. Rossi-Doria, 'Per una storia del 'decentramento conservatore': Antonio di Rudinì e le riforme', *Quaderni Storici*, 18 (September–December 1971).
8. Turiello, *Governo e governati*, 14.
9. P. Villani, *Mezzogiorno tra riforme e rivoluzione* (Bari, 1973), 162.
10. E. C. Banfield, *The Moral Basis of a Backward Society* (New York, 1958).
11. R. Romanelli, 'Political Debate, Social History, and the Italian *borghesia*: Changing Perspectives in Historical Research', *Journal of Modern History*, 63/4 (December 1991), 719, 739.
12. Turiello, *Governo e governati*, 39.
13. Ibid., 42n.

14. A. Anzilotti, 'La cultura politica nella Toscana del Risorgimento e Leopoldo Galeotti (1921)', *Momenti e contrasti per l'unità italiana*, ed., L. Russo (Bari, 1930), 152.

15. P. Turiello, *Governo e governati in Italia* (Bologna, 1889–92), ch. 5, 'Ragione e processo delle instituzioni organiche nei popoli civili' (not present in the Bevilacqua 1980, edn).

16. Letter from E. Falconcini (1860), cited in R. Romanelli, *Sulle carte interminate* (Bologna, 1989), 43.

17. E. Falconcini, *Cinque mesi di prefettura in Sicilia* (Florence, 1863), 18, 98.

18. This term is used in P. Schneider, J. Schneider and E. Hansen, 'Modernization and Development: the Role of Regional Elites and Noncorporate Groups in the European Mediterranean', *Comparative Studies in Society and History*, 14/3 (June 1972), 345, where the authors distinguish between development élites who undertake long-term projects that promote the autonomous development of a region and 'dependence' élites who consume the resources brought into a region but do not themselves generate new ones.

19. *Atti parlamentari: atti della Camera dei Deputati*, Discussioni, tornata de 6 dicembre 1861, (Turin, 1862), 165.

4

The Southern Metropolis
Redistributive Circuits in Nineteenth-century Naples

PAOLO MACRY

A huge head on a weak body

Samuel Langhorne Clemens, better known as Mark Twain, arrived in Naples in the 1860s and was struck by the density of the population, by the half a million people who lived in those four- or five-storey buildings, crammed side by side and divided by dark narrow streets. 'I'm sure that Naples doesn't cover a wider area than an American city of 150,000 inhabitants', he wrote. 'But (and here lies the secret) it soars upwards higher than three American cities put together.'[1]

The English, the Germans and the French who arrived in the city for work or for pleasure, all had the same impression: Naples was hectic, chaotic and noisy, 'the noisiest city in Creation'. Its squares were choked with 'clouds of dust, people and by a deafening noise'. The crowd was 'a turbulent sea, like a torrent that roars in an alpine valley'; it was restless 'like an army of ants', like 'rats in a rat-hole.'[2]

Naples was a metropolis by the mid-nineteenth century: the most densely populated Italian city. It was a completely atypical example in a country that had traditionally been characterized by a network of medium-sized and small cities. Like all the large cities of the time Naples suffered problems of an economic, social and political nature, but here they were exacerbated. The city had long suffered from a sort of chronic Malthusian imbalance. By the end of the sixteenth century Naples—together with London and Paris, the largest European city—was already suffering from an over-large population. Immigrants continued to flock to the city from all parts of Southern Italy, in search of better living conditions. The demographic concentration was out of proportion with the rest of the Kingdom. To use Gaetano Filangeri's metaphor, it was a huge head on a weak body.

The overpopulation of Naples had political rather than economic origins. By the middle of the nineteenth century the city did not present itself as a modern urban centre, sustained by industrial and mercantile development, but, on the contrary, as a densely populated agglomerate, artificially held together.[3] This can be explained by the fact that, for centuries, Naples had been the capital of an absolute state, and in that role had enjoyed fiscal and commercial privileges, subsidized bread, and employment opportunities in the administration of the Kingdom. Attracted by the presence of the court, all the Southern Italian nobility resided in Naples. Here, in their prestigious palaces, they received rent from often distant regions and here they spent most of that revenue (by the middle of the 1800s more than 15,000 servants, cooks, washerwomen, gardeners and coachmen worked for them). In 1845, 20,000 public employees, 18,000 soldiers, 6,000 priests, 2,500 lawyers and barristers worked in Naples—all occupied in employment linked to the political and administrative offices of the capital city.[4] The city teemed with nobles, soldiers, bureaucrats and the poor. It was full of 'parasites', 'hangers-on', 'pettifogging lawyers' and 'adventurers', in the words of Giustino Fortunato.[6] But it did not have an adequate system of production. It was a city that lived beyond its means.

Naples traditionally controlled the entire system of production of the South and was the centre for all the Kingdom's national and international trade. At least until 1860 it was a 'kind of universal emporium of the 8 or 9 million inhabitants of the Kingdom of the Two Sicilies'.[5] Revenues from land, agricultural produce, handicrafts and manufactured goods arrived there from all parts of Southern Italy; what Naples did not consume of these resources was exported to the rest of Italy and Europe.

As the capital and centre of Southern Italy Naples had enjoyed many privileges but, during the 1800s, it lost them. Unification of Italy in 1860 destroyed the city's role as capital, while, since the first decades of the century, some areas of the South had developed their own autonomous economies. This was a dramatic turning point. The large population lost its income and political protection. The Malthusian dilemma became acute: resources were scarce, and popular consumption was under threat. In addition, in the context of the new Italian state, the opportunities for economic development decreased. If we examine the statistics for social mobility in the city in the decades after 1860, we find a system in which social groups were virtually static.[7]

This mixture of population density, weak economic growth and declining 'social protectionism' had important social, economic and cultural repercussions, and resulted in several long-term—or rather structural—features, which can be categorized as follows:

- the city was an enormous system of circulation of resources, which was completely out of proportion to the local production of wealth;
- the system did not seem to be competitive: the market was overstocked (because it absorbed a large amount of staff and capital) and unbalanced (because retailers and producers were controlled by a mercantile élite that often behaved in a monopolistic manner);
- the system did not only respond to the real demand. It also created an artificial demand, by selling 'fake' goods (that is, something which is sold, although it is not produced to be sold) through illegal and often violent means.

We are speaking of a parasitical circuit (a zero-sum circuit of distribution); it exerted great pressure on the city and was characterized by monopolies (legal, illegal and violent) and—as a consequence—by extra benefits.

Shopkeepers and street vendors

Naples was a vast emporium. To the foreign travellers of the 1800s the city appeared to be one large market—a market that did not wait for the client or customer, but sought and pursued him. In 1861, as soon as the German politician Gustav Rasch arrived in the port, he was assailed by boatmen who offered to take him to the quayside. He was made to get onto a coach while 'unknown hands' lifted his luggage onto it. He was then passed on to another stranger who offered him a hotel room and, while the coach went to the hotel, many street vendors stopped it, trying to sell him fruit, freshly squeezed lemonade and flowers.[8] In their diaries these foreign travellers described the people who crowded the large, fragmented, picturesque and informal market. 'The sellers of many different kinds of fruit', Gustav Rasch wrote, 'were squatting down on the narrow pavement, leaning against the buildings; the money lenders were sitting at their tables with piles of money and coppers in front of them; next to these the water vendors were standing by their brightly coloured stalls.'[9] The entire city was a market. The entire population was ready to trade. 'And what can't you buy here?', Ferdinand Gregorovius wondered.[10] Buying and selling was intense in the bourgeois areas, above all in wealthy Via Toledo, where there were both prestigious boutiques and numerous street vendors. It exploded into Piazza Mercato and the narrow streets nearby, where half the agricultural produce from Campania and the catch from the bay arrived. It spread from street to street, building to building, into a dense network of the neighbourhood, into the damp courtyards of street-level slum dwellings, where the sun never penetrated.

Recent historiography has enlarged on the impressions of foreign travellers. Daniela Luigia Caglioti has pointed out the rapid increase in the number of shops and businesses in the nineteenth century.[11] Often they were one-man businesses. In 1871 the city's tertiary sector had an average of 0.7 employees per business; in 1901 the average was 1.2.[12] Premises were often used both for production and for selling; they also served as the shopkeeper's family home—it was a typical family business. If necessary, wives, children, fathers, brothers and sons-in-law worked in the shop, even though this work was considered undignified for women, and where possible their role was hidden. Sons were destined to continue their father's trade (the handing down of a trade from father to son was common). The women's dowries contributed to support the business financially. The family and relatives relied on the shop, obtaining employment and resources from it, and everyone, in times of hardship, 'intervened offering in turn financial and psychological support'.[13] In short, 'the life-cycle of the shopkeeper's family was consumed within the shop itself' and, although the civil code tried to separate the private sphere from the public sphere, there was much confusion between the running of the family and the running of the business.[14] 'Workers' wages and the expenses of child-birth and sickness, the cost of renting the premises, funeral expenses for parents and expenses for mail were systematically mixed in account books which revealed a total ignorance of the most elementary rules of bookkeeping'.[15] The level of literacy of the average shopkeeper was very low. Many of them could not read or write. They could hardly sign the books and they had little knowledge of bookkeeping. What they knew, they had usually learnt from their parents or during an apprenticeship served in another shop: there was 'no comparison with the English tradesmen's schooling and seven-year training'.[16]

For a variety of reasons, the retailers did not enjoy good economic health. In the second half of the nineteenth century the city was in a state of crisis (it had just lost its role as capital) and consumption was rapidly decreasing. Generally speaking, the reduced size of the shops and their excessive number explained the low profits of this category. Furthermore the disastrous effects of a very widespread practice—sales on credit—should not be underestimated. Shopkeepers were obliged to give credit not only to their poorer clients but also to the middle class and the nobility. Here is what a noble, Michele Palmieri di Micciché, wrote about his family's bad (and haughty) habits: 'nous avions effectivement des habits neufs, élégants, mais nous ne payions pas notre tailleur; nous étions parfaitement chaussés, mais nous ne payions pas nos cordonniers; nos chemises et nos cravates étaient de la plus belle et de la plus fine toile, mais nous ne payions pas notre lingère'.[17] All the tradesmen examined by Caglioti had their own long list of outstanding credits, often more theoretical than real, since their collection was so difficult.

The city's enormous demand for food also created a widespread network of street vendors who went back and forth between the city and its nearby agricultural centers: a network unique in Italy at that time. This was a complex system of 'trade which mobilized considerable energies and large economic resources, given the lucrative guaranteed return from a circle of consumption lacking flexibility'.[18] Every day, thanks to the street vendors, 'the countryside literally entered the city': in the streets of Naples, beneath the astonished gaze of foreign travellers, the smallholders brought their goats and cows to be milked in front of their customers;[19] and every day, in the opposite direction, other street vendors went from the city to the villages in the hinterland, to sell cloth and drapery.

Such an overstocked and fragmented market was obviously far from the ideal described by classic economic theory. 'A fixed price—which was the characteristic element of the modern system of commerce—hardly existed in Naples' and the English consul Eustace Neville Rolfe noted that, when shopping, servants and cooks could easily swindle their employers.[20] These small thefts aside, the problem was serious. The absolute lack of fixed prices was the result of a system of exchange that, on the other hand, was fragmentary, short-range and embedded in the social structure, and, on the other, often appeared to be governed by real and effective monopolies.

The shopkeepers and street vendors were organized by a small number of middlemen who financed and controlled them by fair means or foul. In 1861 the pork market, for example, was controlled by only three people, who, according to precise rules, established and shared out the number of animals to be butchered daily so as to prevent a fall in prices. 'The price of meat is very high and this seems to have been caused by a ring of butchers', noted the English consul in 1864.[21] The failure of the efforts made in the second half of the nineteenth century to rationalize the distribution system is significant. In the mid-1860s, for example, the city council employed a French company, the Société des Halles, to build and manage several covered markets. But these new markets never functioned and were closed down soon afterwards. In fact, the regulations and tariffs fixed by the Société des Halles seemed a completely unacceptable novelty. The Neapolitan market depended on unwritten rules, strict power relationships and monopoly positions,[22] and these could not easily be overcome.

The entrepreneurial class: a tertiary vocation?

There was an élite of important merchants, bankers and commissioners behind the shopkeepers and retailers. Historians have unfortunately shown little interest in this tertiary bourgeoisie. With the typical prejudice of latecomers, they have preferred to debate Naples' lack of 'industrial vocation', and have analysed the city's failure to develop industrially despite the apparent presence of many of the presumed prerequisites. Paolo Frascani, however, has recently pointed to a tertiary vocation of the city and 'the aptitude of the Neapolitan entrepreneurial class in the nineteenth century to mediate and exchange rather than produce'. This is 'a real entrepreneurial model, different but not inferior to the industrial model': a model which seems to have come from the centuries of Neapolitan commercial and political domination of Southern Italy.[23]

In 1979 John Davis analysed Neapolitan entrepreneurial skills in the first half of the nineteenth century, noting the large numbers of merchants, bankers, contractors and industrialists, whose fortune depended primarily on the weakness of farmers and shopkeepers, and secondly on political support. These élites worked within a regime of virtual monopoly.[24] 'Thanks to endemic poverty in the primary sector, there was an insatiable hunger for credit, and in particular short-term credit', he noted.[25] Farmers and shopkeepers were dependent on the holders of capital. Agriculture was often controlled by large merchant groups who lent money and seed to small-holders and farmers, imposing heavy conditions.

The political support enjoyed by Neapolitan entrepreneurs during the Bourbon regime was equally important. The state offered its 'friends' among the business community many favourable opportunities. This was not only because the government employed them to build roads and other public works. Due to its own economic difficulties and lack of organization, the state often contracted entire sectors of the market to private businesses, granting exclusive licences for the sale of macaroni and wine, for instance, and even the most important public functions, like the collection of taxes. Needless to say, private businessmen obtained notable secure profits from these state contracts and entry to this much sought after élite was reserved for the chosen few.[26]

After all, Neapolitan industry in the first half of the nineteenth century was kept alive by public orders and the very high excise duties on imported products. The shipyards and metal industry, for example, survived thanks to pro-tectionism and the state's orders for military ships (in 1856 the Bourbon navy had over ninety steam ships).[27] 'Neapolitan manufacturers', John Davis wrote, were the King's men, almost entirely dependent on the sovereign's benevolent protection.[28] Until 1860, it was essential, even for the nobility, to be part of that small and exclusive circle of families in close contact with the court. Recently Giovanni Montroni has listed the many advantages enjoyed by the court nobility—those nobles admitted to the presence of the king—not only prestige but financial benefits. For example, in 1823 the prince of Butera received the monopoly of steamship construction from Ferdinand I, while the prince of Satriano in 1837 obtained a 10-year monopoly for the importation of new machinery for weaving linen and hessian.[29] Even the great and the good showed no disdain for such deals.

Well into the second half of the nineteenth century the city's entrepreneurial class was still affected by its recent past, and in some ways little appeared to have changed since the *ancien régime*. Obviously after 1860 the days of political favours given to the élite attached to the Bourbon regime had come to an end, and this alone was significant. Yet the concentrated and often monopolistic nature of the system of trade had not changed. Neapolitan companies continued to buy crops from agricultural producers before their harvest, paying them in advance. At the same time they financed the retailers, giving them imported goods on short-term credit of a few months. Neapolitan merchants did business with foreign merchants, to whom they sold part of the agricultural yield and from whom they purchased groceries, cloth, and so on.[30] The market continued to be based on severely imbalanced power relationships between the financial–commercial élite and producers. Neapolitan merchants avoided becoming part of the system of agricultural production because of the risks involved, such as the risks of inclement weather, but at the same time they imposed heavy terms on the producers. It is breathtaking to consider the financial and speculative network that traditionally characterized the grain market, and enabled powerful merchants to play the grain market—to buy before the harvest and then speculate on seasonal variations of the price of wheat and, above all, to keep the farmers out of the market.[31]

None the less, towards the end of the century the practice of mediation, based on a monopolistic financing of trade and the exploitation of variations in prices, was progressively abandoned. The most important reasons were the reduction of travelling times; the decline of the port of Naples as the main centre for the export of the Southern agricultural yield; the agrarian crisis and the reorganization of the agricultural activity on which a large part of Neapolitan trade was based; protectionism; and the crisis in the oil and wine markets. The result was the isolation of the city's financial and mercantile élite.

What was the fate of this élite? As experts in trade and speculation, they became involved in playing the market, and particularly in investment in public shares. In fact, the Neapolitan investors of the time seemed 'ready to gamble their resources even in distant and unknown investments'.[32] For example, many Neapolitans owned shares in the Turkish public debt (in 1873 alone, in the city of Naples, shares to the value of 10 million lire were purchased).[33] The size and type of business dealt with in the stock market indicated a model based on pure speculation', Paolo Frascani commented. He also suggested that there was continuity between the commercial and investment activity (often monopolistic and speculative) of the 1860s and 1870s, and a successive tendency towards 'the exploitation of property holdings', continued until the present.[34] Frascani described, for example, the progress of a group of shipowners from Sorrento in the nineteenth century, from maritime trade to building and property developed in the second half of the twentieth century.[35] It is perhaps early to conclude that the entrepreneurs traditionally involved in trade moved *tout court* into the area of property development. But the first indications are there.

After all, if we agree with John Davis' analysis of the first half of the nineteenth century, it is difficult to image how the city's entrepreneurs could later have become 'models of *laissez-faire* or part of a liberal leadership.[36] What real opportunities did Naples offer them? The poor prospects for industrial growth, and therefore the lack of opportunity for productive investment, have already been mentioned. But the choices of the city's mercantile élite should be considered in the light of the high earnings deriving from the supra-profits that the traditional gaps in the market had always guaranteed to the so-called 'Neapolitan monopolists'. Their choices were influenced by the extremely profitable earnings that could be had in realty. The high density of inhabitants in the city led to a chronic imbalance between supply and demand in the housing market and therefore the remuneration from property was always very high. The fact is that property construction and property investment attracted a large amount of capital and entrepreneurial ability away from other less well-proven and riskier forms of investment. In a context of monopolistic earnings derived from positions obtained by privilege, one cannot expect the city's élite to worry about changing their financial investments.

John Davis, referring to the first half of the nineteenth century, pointed out that 'investment in poverty was remunerative' and therefore, 'if Neapolitan businessmen had tried to invest their capital in a more adventurous and modern way, not only would they have had to accept a lower and less secure return but they would have acted irrationally, to use Weber's term'.[37] In the second half of the nineteenth century the days of privileges and monopolies had come to an end—but not entirely: there did not yet seem to be an alternative to the logic of living off capital.

There is one last point to consider regarding this situation. Even without being excessively optimistic about the modern market and open society, we can reasonably say that a system that was encumbered by earnings from status, like the one in nineteenth-century Naples, contributed to making social diversions more rigid. In some ways, for example, income from trade required 'membership' of that class: it was an inaccessible privilege—a fact well-reflected in the continuity of Neapolitan trade dynasties from the eighteenth to the nineteenth century. Naples—as the literature of the nineteenth century had emphasized—was the home of acute sociological and topographical divisions, despite appearances to the contrary. The imbalance of the city's market confirmed this.

Credit, usury and realty

The credit system extended far beyond the unilateral relations between merchants and bankers on the one hand and retailers and farmers on the other, in which the former dictated to the latter. The credit system was much broader. It was another fragmented and overcrowded redistributive sector. As a result of the lack of a modern network of banks, private loans were widespread and involved individuals and families, men and women, lower and upper classes, legal and illegal networks.

Study of the Neapolitan élite of the late nineteenth century, its family system and its estates, has revealed that many wives would invest their dowry in moneylending activities (daughters from élite families were usually given money as a dowry by their fathers, while sons were given realty). Other moneylenders were state contractors, the tertiary, middle-class property-holders. They were men and women who, having chosen to invest their money in the credit circuit, could obtain

8–11 per cent interest—much more than the interest available on shares in the public debt.[38] More historical research is needed on this matter.

What can be said, however, is that credit was one of the keystones of the Neapolitan distributive system. It determined a wide and rapid circulation of realty. Credit was often used to obtain property from the debtor, if he was not able to repay the debt on time. The composition of creditors' estates revealed by documents of Neapolitan notaries is significant: these estates comprised dozens of small flats, sheds, storerooms, shops, and so on. They were the result of loans which had not been repaid: lending money meant obtaining realty, and in this way Naples was passed from hand to hand.[39] Here is another radical and entrenched exploitation of the gaps in the market.

The system of credit also had an illegal side. Usury was very common practice in nineteenth-century Naples, a product of poverty and the imbalance of the city's financial market. Pauperism was severe and diffuse. Significantly, in 1861 the Bank of Naples opened a special pawnshop where people—or rather, women—could pawn the so-called *pannine*, that is their bed linen and table linen. Naples was, of course, full of private pawnshops.[40] The fact is that the survival of the lower classes was based on debts and on the continuous postponement of their repayment. However, the middle classes also suffered from the scarcity of money and banks, and Carolina Castellano has established that the victims of usury in the late nineteenth century included hairdressers, dentists, teachers and respectable ladies.[41] Naples provided a particularly favourable environment for the diffusion of usury. People needed money and had no alternative but to accept the high rates of interest that were imposed. But the usury chain was very hard to break. It was difficult to pay such high rates of interest. In the 1880s, for example, a woman received 200 lire from a neighbour (another woman). Some years later, despite the fact that the debtor had payed a part of the interest, the loan had reached the sum of 700 lire. At that moment, the debtor was paying the creditor one lira a week, 52 lire a year.[42] Needless to say, it would have been very difficult and frequently impossible ever to extinguish such a loan.

The market in 'fake' administrative goods

The system of distribution did not only serve to supply goods according to demand, but it produced a market by creating a demand for and selling 'fake' goods.

This is what happened in the administrative sector. In 1901 a special commission, set up to investigate corruption in the city council of Naples under Guiseppe Saredo, revealed that the entire city was enmeshed in a web of political favours. In exchange for money, a band of intermediaries accepted the role of mediator 'between the citizen and Justice, the citizen and Authority, the citizen and the Administration, the citizen and the Bank'.[43] In other words, there was in Naples a market for the purchase of public administration services which should, in theory, have been free and neutral. Saredo commented:

> From the rich industrialist who sought to enter the political or administrative class to the small trader who required a reduction in duties, from the businessman who hoped for a contract to the workman looking for a job, from the professional hoping to pick up clients from some public body to anyone seeking a clerical post . . . all of them were approached by a mediator (the so called *interposta persona*) and nearly all accepted.[44]

Even the legal administration was afflicted by this obviously illegal band of intermediaries who operated between the clients, the lawyers and the judges themselves (to the extent that Saredo proposed that, in Naples, the judiciary should not be composed of Neapolitans).[45] This system of mediation made public functions, from the most modest to the most important, part of a market, and thus 'whatever was a right became a favour'.[46] This was the system that created and sold 'fake' goods.

This phenomenon of corruption of course existed in other parts of Italy and Europe, but in Naples it was particularly widespread and created an enormous web. There, wrote Francesco Saveri Nitti, for one reason or another, 50,000 people were obliged to deal with the city council.[47] The extent

of the corruption produced remarkable effects. First, it became
a significant burden on family income and it was a system that
distributed wealth and created jobs. Second, the sales of
administrative services increased the numbers of mediators:
just as there was a surplus of traders and shopkeepers who
extended the line from production to consumption, so every
transaction between a citizen and a public body was burdened
by the presence of mediators. Third, the inevitable result of
corruption was a loss of the trust in the institutions and their
neutrality that had been the pride and joy (at least in theory)
of nineteenth-century Liberalism. Indeed, in Naples it was not
unusual that employment in public administration was an
instrument for the realization of other objectives. Nitti
commented, 'Local administrative posts are given to people
who use them for their own career.' If one considers the mass
of 5,000 or 6,000 lawyers living in the city at the end of the
nineteenth century, it is clear, Nitti says, 'that those who are at
the beginning of their career use the career ladder of local
government as a mean to establish themselves. The *comune*
gives them the chance to grant many favours and pick up
clients.[48] In short, political and administrative posts became 'a
way of feathering their own nests'.[49]

The market of the *camorra*

There was another distributive circuit for 'unreal' goods, which
should not be forgotten: namely that created by the Neapolitan
mafia known as the *camorra*. The *camorra* penetrated the city's
market: it was its own special market, where supply created its
own demand and not vice versa. In some ways this phenomenon symbolizes and links the different elements discussed
so far: the *camorra* was closely linked to the city's large food
market; it was a business and it followed entrepreneurial
patterns; it was a typically monopolistic system: it was the
result of the state's weakness and the inefficiency of the
enforcement of state law. Marcello Marmo's recent works have
illustrated this phenomenon.[50]

The *camorra* was a criminal organization, which obtained its wealth, for the most part, in two ways: by running illegal operations (prostitution, gambling, clandestine numbers games, smuggling) and through extortion. It was rooted in the prisons and lower-class areas of the city: it was essentially a plebeian phenomenon and remained so for decades (in contrast with the *mafia*, which typically brings together lower and higher classes, and even the ruling class). In the second half of the nineteenth century, in the slums of Vicaria, Mercato and Porto, there were about twenty-five or thirty active *camorra* members per 10,000 inhabitants, while in the respectable areas of San Ferdinand or Avvocata, there were no more than between five and eight.[51]

Diego Gambetta has pointed out that organized crime (like the *mafia* and the *camorra*) sells goods of a special nature—goods that are produced in competition with the state and that provide a substitute for public order: private protection.[52] While it is true that the *camorra* had a role as a means of law enforcement since it disciplined and controlled the widespread delinquency in the city and the criminal violence towards people and property, nevertheless it only fulfilled a pre-existing need for trust to a limited extent. For the most part it was the *camorra* itself that created a certain level of disorder and violence, thereby creating the need for public order and private protection. In other words, the *camorra* sold goods (trust) for which it had created the need, through 'an injection of measured doses of distrust'.[53]

Trust and the lack of it were manipulated by the *camorra* using violent means. Obviously such violence can only be considered in relation to the weakness and connivance of the authorities, and the fact that public authority itself used the *camorra* to control the city. In 1860, with the collapse of the Bourbon regime and on the eve of Garibaldi's entry into the city, the prefect of Naples, Liborio Romano, asked the *camorra* bosses to guarantee public order in exchange for the inclusion of some *camorra* members in the police force.[54] The consequences of the Romano-*camorra* agreement—which lasted some months—were, on the one hand, the efficient social control of the city and, on the other, 'the considerable escalation of crime, thanks to the protection of the police uniform'.[55]

The *camorra* and the market were inextricably linked, both because the *camorra* managed whole sectors of the market (wholesale foodstuffs, smuggling) and because its extortion racket affected the entire market. The payment of protection money was extorted from practically 'all the areas of the market, whether legal or illegal'—fruit, meat, grain and flour, fish, the workshops, all kinds of transport (wagons and carriages, porters, boats and ships), usury, places of *sociabilité* (coffee shops, taverns and gambling dens), street gambling, popular street celebrations, the brothels, the beggars. The *camorra* extorted money in exchange for protection wherever there was a market or a power relationship existed.[56]

As Marcella Marmo has highlighted, the activity of the *camorra* resembled that of the beggar or mediator rather than that of the thief.[57] Also, I would suggest, it resembled the activity of the monopolistic businessmen of the early nineteenth century, who manipulated the law as they pleased, attracting a large clientele through state money. But *camorra* extortion was also a clear imitation of the fiscal system—a taxation system that formerly in the South of Italy had been identified with the looting carried out by the Spanish army, the extortion exercised by the barons (itself of dubious legality), the extortion of the numerous thugs, or the traditional extortion inflicted by the police on shopkeepers or prostitutes.[58]

And of course this was an entrepreneurial activity that was both complex and well organized. The *camorra* efficiently blackmailed an entire system of exchange. '*Facimm caccià l'oro de' piducchie*' ('We can even get gold from lice'), a *camorra* boss stated proudly in the mid-nineteenth century,[59] meaning that the *camorra* controlled every transaction in the city, even the most modest, from the deals of large mercantile monopolies to the begging of vagrants in the street. Consider what happened in a classic *camorra* stronghold—the nineteenth century prison:

> As soon as they arrive, the new prisoners have to sell their clothes and food assigned by the prison to the camorra at

ridiculous prices. In turn the camorra boss resells them to the prison suppliers (who thus save on replenishment) while the prisoners are forced to gamble the little money they receive from the sale and to buy a bottle of wine for the camorra boss . . .

who had—of course—a monopoly on gambling and on the sale of wine in prison. As if this were not enough, the *camorra* imposed an extra tax of 10 per cent on all goods and services available in prison (food and clothes brought by relatives, haircuts, lawyers' visits, and so on).[60] The striking thing is that out of nothing was created a stable circuit of exchange—or rather the real circulation of money—even in prison.

At a cultural level the *camorra* system—like the administrative corruption—gave rise to a lack of trust in public services, which elsewhere were guaranteed by the state, resulting in individualistic behaviour. Even more than in Olson's metaphor of the 'free rider', the only way out seems always to have been private, never public, always individual, never universal. Giuseppe Saredo identified in Naples 'an individualism developed to such an extent that it had no equal in others parts of Italy', a chronic 'isolation of individuals' and, in consequence, the importance of 'a family that encompassed all the desires of the individual'. Perhaps these are generalizations affected by the prejudices of external observers (Saredo was from Liguria). However the fact remains that a consistent element of Neapolitan culture appears to have been—and still to be today—a sort of communication gap, in the sense intended by Jürgen Habermas.[61]

The usury banks

The city's market was weighed down by a series of zero-sum distributive circuits. In Naples, zero-sum distribution influenced the city's wealth and its social fabric, but it was also—and above all—a widespread cultural phenomenon. It was characterized by the constant expectation of an effortless acquisition of wealth or, conversely, of obtaining gold from lice, by defying the laws of economics.

Let us consider a little known but significant event, namely the phenomenon of the usury banks.[62] In 1866 the Italian government suspended the convertibility of banknotes, resulting in an increase of the value of gold compared with paper money. In Naples a certain Guglielmo Ruffo dei Principi di Scilla (a nobleman? an imposter?) profited from this decline in the lira's prestige and began to collect money from small savers. In return he offered to repay the sum twenty days later in gold. In other words, he promised a high interest rate, which was far above the market rate. This operation was rather successful and was to continue for three years. In fact, the banker earned the trust of investors, managing to pay the promised interest on time. This was a game based on the mere circulation of money. Guglielmo Ruffo paid the interest with the very capital that had been deposited. The circulation of money could be maintained only if the influx of new capital continued.

His example, of course, was followed by other financiers of varying capabilities. At the beginning of 1870, in the space of only a few weeks, more than a hundred new banks were set up in Naples! But, having to compete with one another, they were forced to offer ever increasing interest rates to potential savers: 15 per cent per month, then 18 per cent, then 20 per cent, then 30 per cent . . . such interest rates were as incredible as they were tempting. The race was on. As the number of banks increased, so the interest rates went up, and as the interest rates went up, so more people deposited their savings. The banks (which by now were called usury banks, as the interest rates offered were typical of usury) managed in this way to accumulate rapidly unheard-of-sums of money. When the bubble burst in February 1870, it was discovered that over 10,000 savers had deposited money and the deficit was more than 40 million lire! This was an enormous amount of money, which had for the most part been deposited in the few weeks before the crash. The fact that at this point the capital of the Bank of Naples was 27 million lire gives some idea of the significance of this sum.[63]

The usury banks crashed as rapidly as they had appeared, of course. The flow of money entering the banks had only to slow down for the banks to find it impossible to pay the interest. In turn, unpaid interest caused distrust in savers, who stopped investing and asked to withdraw the capital deposited. An abrupt end.

This event reveals a collective way of behaviour that it would be superficial to define as irrational. The prefect of Naples explained it, in a letter written to the Interior Minister after the crash: 'For everyone it was like gambling, like a risk to be faced, like a race in which you hope to finish first, leaving the others by the wayside.[64] A zero-sum game of chance. The usury banks limited themselves to the distribution of resources by transferring them from one saver to another at an ever increasing pace. And everyone seemed to understand the process. Every saver knew that the interest he received came from the money deposited by other savers. And, in fact, when the crash came, no one seemed to be very surprised. It was clear that, sooner or later, the bubble would have burst. Was it collective folly? Or was folly only in the same sense as gambling; rather, it was like betting against time. Just as in a race, everyone knew that whoever came last would be the loser with the usury banks.

As Marcella Marmo has suggested, this event reflects several Neapolitan characteristics: a city full of large and small amounts of unused capital, a city without formal economics or industrial development, a city accustomed to other types of parasitic behaviour such as speculation, usury, *camorra* extortion, pickpocketing and numerous petty crimes against property. Naturally such behaviour did not create wealth but merely moved it around between individuals. A kind of 'moral economy of redistribution'[65] but, not, of course, an egalitarian redistribution.

It is interesting to examine what happened immediately after the crash. Some people suggested that the capital still available should be returned to the creditors of the usury banks, not in proportion to their credits, but through a lottery to be organized by the Bank of Naples. The few lucky winners would recuperate their savings. Yet another risk, yet another gamble.

Gambling

The proposal of a lottery would not have sounded strange to Neapolitan ears. It must be interpreted within the context of a centuries-old Neapolitan tradition: gambling.[66] Gambling too, incidentally, was traditionally linked to the market and was very widespread in mercantile cities such as Naples, Genoa and Venice, and popular in the merchant class. In the early modern age, for example, Neapolitan merchants bet on the price of wheat after the harvest—another example of the opportunities taken to play the grain market.

And so Naples was the gambling capital of Italy. In Naples every type of game was played everywhere: in the streets, in the taverns, in the prisons, in the theatres, in the churches, in the courthouse—cards, dice and above all, from the end of the seventeenth century, the state lottery: the *lotto*. The popularity, the spread, the collective character of the *lotto*, and the redistributive system it created are particularly striking. Between the second half of the eighteenth century and the first half of the nineteenth in a city of 300,000–400,000 inhabitants, 400,000–500,000 bets were placed every week—an incredible ratio of more than one per head! The *lotto* ignored class differences. It was played by the élites (the Bourbons too) and by the lower classes. Even if the average sum of money wagered was clearly very low, the extent of participation among Neapolitans meant that there was an enormous capital sum involved. During the Bourbon years the organization of the *lotto* was one of the main financial operations of the state.

The *lotto* produced a continuous circulation of money. From 1750 to 1850 almost half the amount placed in bets was returned as winnings. They were usually modest winnings, but all the same they resulted in a significant movement of money. This cannot even be described as yet one more example of zero-sum redistribution: the *lotto* was a kind of collective self-taxation (a voluntary tax, as the economists of the time called it), given that the bookmaker did not pay the winners according to statistical probability, but much less. In the long term, therefore, the state was guaranteed a secure and constant profit: about 50 per cent of the money bet. Clearly this did not stop the practice. It was a social custom with strong cultural connotations. It was a tradition expressed in rituals that Neapolitans were not willing to change in the slightest. *Noli me tangere* was the motto of the state bookmakers, when faced with various proposals to rationalize a system burdened with highly complex rules. The French lottery, for example, was much more straightforward. In Naples, the *lotto* was a ritual that could not be modernized.

Can the *lotto* really be classed as a form of gambling? It was a betting game based on chance but above all on an attempt to analyse and interpret the future. The art of prediction and the analysis of dreams was much more common than playing a system or random bets. In fact the game was not based on chance but required specialist skills and precise knowledge. The winner was a hero, a sage, a saint, a wizard. Giustino Fortunato wrote, as 'the winnings themselves were nothing if not the result of constancy, of skill and of cabalistic doctrine.'[67]

Also, the *lotto* circuit was strictly linked to the whole distributive system. The clandestine *lotto*, the so-called 'small game', was very diffuse in nineteenth-century Naples. The 'small game' was played through a widespread network of private and illegal bookmakers. Bets were collected street by street, neighbourhood by neighbourhood, and were based on the personal trust between those who placed the bets and the bookmakers. Needless to say, the 'small game' was controlled by the *camorra*.[68] The *lotto* was a circuit in which legal and illegal behaviours, legal and illegal ethics, tended to be mingled. Sometimes the bookmakers of the state lottery and the private bookmakers of the 'small game' were one and the same person. Besides, the gambling circuit was connected at its base to the cycle of usury. Here is what an author wrote about this matter in 1907:

> It is on Friday, that day when all Neapolitan people *deve fare 'e vigliette* [must bet on the *lotto*], it is on 'greedy Friday' that subtle and destructive usury is perpetuated. People who lack a penny to buy a bit of bread ... *must* find at all cost twenty, thirty pence to try their luck. And the small usurer is there, ready, lying in wait.[69]

Trade, *camorra*, usury, gambling: these circuits seem always to be connected with each other. The one is ruled by the other. The one is financed by the other.

The complex Neapolitan system of redistribution was therefore entangled with monopolies, speculation, extortion, administrative corruption and also with a tradition of gambling and divination. In Naples, characterized by social rigidity and rifts between different groups, professions and cultures, communication took place within these redistribution circuits, through formal and informal, legal and illegal, contacts. Such idiosyncrasies could, and indeed do, provide interesting material for an anthropologist or an historian, but they did not favour the production of social wealth. After all, Naples has always been characterized—and is still so today—by a scarcity of public goods and thus by a scarcity of public ethics.

NOTES

1. In various authors, *Viaggiatori del Grand Tour in Italia* (Milan, 1987).
2. G. Rasch, *Garibaldi a Napoli nel 1860. Note di un viaggiatore prussiano* (Bari, 1938), 40, 45; F. Gregorovius, *Napoli* (Naples, 1892), 30; H. Taine, *Viaggio in Italia* (Turin, 1932), 32; W.J. Stamer, *'Dolce Napoli'. Naples: its streets, people, fêtes, pilgrimages, environs* (London, 1878), 38.
3. G. Galasso, *Mezzogiorno medievale e moderno* (Turin, 1965), 401.
4. G. Galasso, 'Professioni, arti e mestieri della popolazione di Napoli nel sec XIX', *Annuario dell'Istituto Storico per l'età moderna e contemporanea*, 13–14 (1961–2).
5. Alfredo Cottrau, quoted in F.S. Nitti, *La città di Napoli* (Naples, 1902), 17.
6. G. Fortunato, *Scritti varii* (Florence, 1928), 193.
7. G. Laurita, 'Comportamenti matrimoniali e mobilità sociale a Napoli', *Quaderni Storici*, 56 (1984).
8. Rasch, *Garibaldi*, 38–42.
9. Ibid., 48.
10. Gregorovius, *Napoli*, 30.
11. D.L. Caglioti, 'Artigiani e dettaglianti in citta' in P. Macry and P. Villani, eds, *La Campania* (Turin, 1990); D.L. Caglioti, 'Mobilià sociale e mobilità geografica. Il piccolo commercio napoletano (1860–1888)', *Meridiana* 17 (1993); D.L. Caglioti, *Il guadagno difficile. I commercianti napoletani nella seconda metà dell'Ottocento* (Bologna, 1994).
12. Caglioti, 'Artigiani e dettaglianti', 671.
13. Ibid., 686.
14. Ibid., 678.
15. Ibid., 680.
16. Ibid., 669.

17. P. Macry, *Ottocento. Famiglia, élites e patrimoni e Napoli* (Turin, 1988), 212.
18. P. Frascani, 'Mercato e commercio a Napoli dopo l'Unità', in P. Macry and P. Villani, eds, *La Campania*, 196.
19. Caglioti, 'Artigiani e dettaglianti', 673.
20. Ibid., 672.
21. Frascani, 'Mercato', 197.
22. Ibid.
23. Ibid., 186–87.
24. J. Davis, *Società e imprenditori nel regno borbonico, 1815–1860* (Bari, 1979).
25. Ibid., 32.
26. Ibid., 172.
27. Ibid., 112.
28. Ibid., 128.
29. G. Montroni, 'I gentiluomini della chiave d'oro', *Meridiana*, 19 (1994), 72–5.
30. Frascani, 'Mercato', 214.
31. Ibid., 210; P. Macry, 'Ceto mercantile e azienda agricola nel Regno di Napoli: il contratto alla voce nel XVIII secolo', *Quaderni Storici*, 21 (1972); P. Macry, *Mercato e società nel Regno di Napoli. Commercio del grano e politica economica nel Settecento* (Naples, 1974).
32. Frascani, 'Mercato', 212.
33. Ibid.
34. Ibid.
35. Ibid., 186–87.
36. Davis, *Società, 128*.
37. *Ibid., 321.*
38. *Macry,* Ottocento, ch. 4.
39. Ibid.
40. G. Imbucci, *Per una storia della povertà a Napoli* (Naples, 1985).
41. C. Castellano, 'La mercantessa e la mediatrice. Storia di un circuito usuraio nella Napoli di fine '800', *Quaderni Storici*, 83 (1993), 586.
42. Ibid., 568.
43. R. Commissione d'Inchiesta per Napoli, *Relazione sull'amministrazione comunale*, 1 (Rome, 1901).
44. Ibid., 50.
45. Ibid., 52.
46. Ibid., 51.
47. L. Musella, *Individui, amici, clienti. Relazione personali e circuiti politici in Italia meridionale tra Otto e Novecento* (Bologna, 1994), 161.
48. Ibid., 167.
49. Rocco de Zerbi, quoted in R. Commissione d'Inchiesta, *Relazione*, 49.
50. M. Marmo, ed., 'Mafia e camorra: storici a confronto', special issue of *Quaderni del Dipartimento di Scienze Sociali dell'Istituto Universitario Orientale*, 2 (1988); M. Marmo, 'La camorra e lo stato liberale, *Camorra e criminalità organizzata in Campania*, ed., F. Barbagallo (Naples, 1988); M. Marmo 'L'onore dei violenti, l'onore delle vittime. Un'estorsione camorrista del 1862 a Napoli', *Onore e storia nelle società mediterranee*, ed., G. Fiume (Palermo, 1989); M. Marmo, 'Tra le carceri e i mercati.

68

82 PAOLO MACRY

Spazi e modelli storici del fenomeno camorrista', *La Campania*, eds Macry and Villani; 'Alla ricerca delle funzioni. Aspetti di ordine e disordine sociale nella camorra napoletana', *Meridiana*, 7—8 (1990).
51. Marmo, *Tra le carceri*, 697.
52. D. Gambetta, 'Mafia: i costi della sfiducia', *Le strategie della fiducia. Indagine sulla razionalità della cooperazione*, ed., D. Gambetta (Turin, 1989).
53. Marmo, *Tra le carceri*, 725.
54. P. Macry, 'Notables, professions libérales, employés: la difficile identité des bourgeoisies italiennes dans la deuxième moitié du XIXe siècle, *Mélanges de l'ecole Française de Rome* (MEFRM), 97/1 (1985), 341–42.
55. Marmo, 'Tra le carceri', 701.
56. Ibid., 694, 714.
57. Ibid., 715.
58. Ibid., 713–14.
59. Ibid., 715.
60. Ibid., 712.
61. S. Maffettone, 'Un'etica pubblica per il Mezzogiorno', *Delta*, 64 (1994).
62. M. Marmo, 'La strana forma del credito. Cultura urbana e autorità liberale nella vicenda delle banche-usura', *Fra storia e storiografia. Scritti in onore di Pasquale Villani*, eds, P. Macry and A. Massasafra (Bologna, 1994); G. Moricola, 'Usurai, prestatori, banchieri. Aspetti delle relazioni creditizie in Campania durante l'Ottocento', *La Campania*, eds, Macry and Villari, 643–44.
63. Marmo, 'La strana forma', 791.
64. Ibid., 792.
65. Ibid., 806.
66. This paragraph is based on research I am completing on gambling and the *lotto* in eighteenth- and nineteenth-century Naples (figures and quotations are from Archivo di Stato di Napoli, Fondo del Ministero delle Finanze).
67. G. Fortunato, *Scritti varii* (Florence, 1928), 213.
68. G. Machetti, 'Le leggi eccezionali post-unitarie e la repressione della camorra: un problema di ordine pubblico?, *Camorra*, ed., Barbagallo, 35.
69. Quoted in Castellano, 'La mercantessa', 569.

5

Images of the South
The *Mezzogiorno* as seen by Insiders and Outsiders

GABRIELLA GRIBAUDI

The Southern question (*questione meridionale*) continues to be discussed as a clearly defined subject rather than as a set of controversial historical constructs.[1] This chapter starts from the conviction that a subject can only be understood if the processes through which that subject's image has been created are analysed, in this case processes in which the dialogue between North and South has played a crucial part. The particular conditions in which this dialogue has been conducted have reflected the imbalance between the two parties involved. It may seem obvious that the idea and therefore the identity of the South of Italy (*Sud, Mezzogiorno, Meridione*) has been moulded through its dialogue with the North, yet the various works which have been published on this subject rarely take this factor into consideration.

An identity is the product of a comparison. Whenever an 'Other' is imagined, the bases of the concept are the categories and images that reflect the culture of a familiar society and that 'Other' is translated into terms with which one is already acquainted. Anyone wishing to represent him- or herself chooses from the authentic and constitutive elements of his or her social group only those elements that serve to advance understanding, to send a message, to affirm a position of power, or to accept a position of subordination. The phenomenon has been studied at various levels: with respect to the formation of individual and group identities in relation to reference groups,[2] the aspects of social differentiation that accompany social mobility,[3] and communication between different cultures.[4] Symbols and images contribute as much to the formation of individual and group identity as material variables. If one is not aware of this, there is the risk of accepting as real data images that are rooted in mental perceptions.

Deconstructionism too places the idea of 'interpretation' and the 'representation' of the Other at the centre of its concerns. It is well known that it urges the denial of all reference to the real: an object only exists in representation. This line of enquiry leads to realms of philosophical debate beyond the scope of this chapter. Suffice it to say that if it is controversial to state that objects only exist in representation, one can agree with the proposition that some objects more than others are the product of mental and ideological elaboration. In such instances, and this is the case with the *Mezzogiorno*, reality and representation combine inextricably—the object is defined by the language chosen for analysis and it is therefore necessary to 'deconstruct' the images and logic that have defined it. North and South have interpreted each other through scientific paradigms and pre-existing stereotypes; they have exchanged images and interpretations, fashioning their respective identities by reflecting one another. If one ignores this element, these interactive mechanisms which have created the images, and fails to place them in their cultural and historical context, one will understand little about the questions relating to the history of the South. The South is much more than a geographical area. It is a metaphor which refers to an imaginary and mythical entity, associated with both hell and paradise: it is a place of the soul and an emblem of the evil that occurs everywhere, but an emblem that in Italy has been embodied in just one part of the nation's territory, becoming one of the myths on which the nation has been built.

In 1860, the lands belonging to the Kingdom of the Two Sicilies which became part of the unified nation were in a weak position and were obliged to measure themselves against cultural and economic models based on profoundly different societies. This argument could be applied to the whole of Italy but it has particular relevance in explaining the situation of the *Mezzogiorno*.[5] The region's identity was in fact based on negation, on what it lacked in relation to the ideal model: a bourgeoisie, an entrepreneurial class, middle strata, individualism, group solidarity. The cultural features of Southern Italy had great difficulty in obtaining any positive recognition in the founding myths of the Italian nation, apart from abstract references to its Greek and Roman past. Its history was treated as a dark age, whose worst expression was to be found in its rule by the Spanish viceroys and the Bourbons. Meanwhile, nineteenth-century Italy sought the roots of a possible national identity in the history of the medieval city states and the Renaissance, with its art, its great men and the Italian (Tuscan) language. Naturally, the South was excluded from this history and the models to which it appealed. The classical ideal expressed by the Florence of the Medici constituted a positive ideal for the nation and one which every community in Italy had to measure up to. This attitude was found in *Napoli a occhio nudo* by the Tuscan writer Renato Fucini, who belonged to the circle of Pasquale Villari. In 1877 he described the monuments of Naples in the following way:

> No other city in the world I believe equals Naples in conserving such paltry and insignificant architectural remains from the successive dynasties that have ruled over her. Of the Byzantines and Normans there is the occasional and shapeless relic. The Swabians and Angevins have left a few churches but their solid palaces resemble sturdy fortresses rather than princely residences. To the Spanish is owed an abundance of awkward-looking churches and the odd obscenely baroque obelisk. The royal palaces of the Bourbons are only worthy of the name on account of their dimensions and on the outside as on the inside they are no more than ordinary houses on a colossal scale.

And the model or ideal for Fucini is provided by 'the revered spirits of Palladio, Scamozzi, Ammannati, and the long line of great men whose splendid example has been so neglected in recent times'.[6]

In the concluding remarks of Benedetto Croce's *Storia del regno di Napoli* (1925)—in many ways a reassessment of the history of the South—we find:

> It has been said that 'Italy ends at the Garigliano', and such is the opinion of travellers and tourists coming from the northern and central regions, who expect to find great natural beauties and ruins of Greek and Roman antiquity but none of the glorious monuments of Italian history or the works of a famous school of art such as they have admired elsewhere. Beside the masterpieces of Tuscan, Lombard, and Venetian artists that were created or brought here by chance, they find, for the most part, secondary works, ostentatious rather than of intrinsic worth. Historians of classical Italian literature, also, are little concerned with Southern Italy, which boasts no Dante, Machiavelli or Ariosto. The South is almost extraneous to the second wave of civilization (the first being that of ancient Rome) which radiated from the Italian peninsula between the beginning of the communes and the height of the Renaissance.[7]

It is significant that after 1946 the South was excluded from the myth on which the Italian Republic was founded, that of the resistance movement. While in the North a part of the population had fought in 1943–5 against German domination and what remained of Italian Fascism, the South had been subjected to Allied occupation. Thus once again the citizens of the South found themselves obliged after the war to celebrate and mythologize an event—the resistance—in which they had not been able to participate. The continued support for monarchism in the South—the extreme defence of the nation's identity through the sovereign—and the subsequent powerful attachment to local myths and identities, can perhaps be explained by the inability to identify with events and actions which could not be experienced at first hand.

The invention of borders

When, in the early 1990s a large banner with the words 'Welcome to Europe' was held aloft at the Sunday football match in Milan's San Siro stadium to greet fans of the visiting team, Naples, the latter responded at the return match with a banner that read 'Turin, Milan, Verona. Give us Africa'. Football fans were among the first to take up the arms of territorial dispute again, especially at a time when Naples was competing successfully with the best Northern clubs. By doing so they were unconsciously resurrecting a very old set of questions regarding borders. The question of borders resurfaced with the rise of the Lega Lombarda, a party that has demanded the division of Italy into three macro-regions. Any record of everyday conversations would carry references to it. Look at popular television shows and one has a good chance of finding jokes about walls designed to divide Italy. If one goes back in time, history is full of similar images. Nor are they exclusive to popular culture; popular and 'high cultural' images intermingle. The vicious, or virtuous, circle, depending on one's point of view, has produced an under-current of stock phrases and scientific categories and symbols that are drawn on in moments of conflict, revealing patterns of recurrence.

'Europe ends at Naples and ends badly. Calabria, Sicily and all the rest belong to Africa', wrote Creuzé de Lesser in 1806. The South was considered a frontier dividing civilized Europe from countries populated by savages from Africa—as in the image used by the football fans. The frontier was also shifting: it could be the Garigliano river, once the border between the Kingdom of Naples and the Papal States, or Naples the last city, or Nocera the end of the railway line, or Eboli the last stage of the postal service.[8] The proverb from which Carlo Levi took the title of his famous book *Cristo si è fermato a Eboli* meant precisely that: beyond Eboli was a land inhabited by savages whose redemption not even Christ through his presence had been able to achieve.[9] The border was so distinct and impassable that Christ had not reached that far, leaving the area outside history, immersed in a kind of static order—a peasant civilization that remained prehistoric and pagan. Naples dismayed travellers, but it was a city. For some it was disturbing and marvellous, and for others frightening and terrible, yet it was one of Italy's great cities. After Naples one fell into an abyss, an inferno, an outpost of Africa. On the other hand, the myth of the savage could assume positive connotations of nobility with changes in taste and cultural preference.[10] For the travellers who undertook the journey south under the influence of Rousseau, the South represented the mythical state of nature, a primitive and savage world untouched by and opposed to Europe's stale and artificial civilization. 'The journey to the South is a sentimental adventure, an adventure of the spirit and an encounter with a very different world; it is a journey in search of yourself, of your authentic self, freed of the layers of superimposed manners and constraints.[11]

During this period the South appeared to be a 'paradise inhabited by devils'. The South was a marvellous and happy land, while the inhabitants were savages. The immoral behaviour and the lack of civilization were precisely the product of the climate and the pleasant and attractive country-side which made it possible to live in a state of nature, a primitive contentment allowing only for the most extreme and basic passions. The bounteous climate induced laziness, inertia and a lack of responsibility, and promoted the supremacy of nature over history and civilization. The people of the North, on the other hand, were accustomed to the struggle with nature, pitting against nature the forces of enterprise, sacrifice and will-power.

Unification and the late nineteenth century

When the Piedmontese administrators went south, they carried these images with them. The South was a happy land, kissed by the gods, favoured by the climate and the fruitfulness of the soil. Yet violence and anarchy reigned there because of the former rulers, the Bourbons. The good, rationalizing, honest Piedmontese administration was going to solve everything. Once the tumour of Bourbon corruption had been excised, everything would return to the gentle and happy state promised by the natural environment. When the Piedmontese realized that the Southerners were rebelling against them and rejecting them, they changed their tune and reverted to the idea of a paradise inhabited by devils: the South as a happy land rendered unhappy by men. Civilization had to be imposed on the inhabitants even at gunpoint, otherwise the cancer represented by the Southerners' behaviour would spread and infect the rest of the nation.[12] The conflict between the two parts of the country increased in the early years after Unification. The ruling class of the North showed a total lack of understanding of the culture and institutions of the South. There was also the problem of obtaining popular legitimation for the new political system, which added to existing and long-standing problems like brigandage, dealt with by military occupation. In this case, as Moe has shown, the image of the Southerners as devils was particularly suited to the measures taken against them.

Then the territorial conflict was superimposed on other types of conflict. First of all, there was the conflict between the Historic Right and the Savoy monarchy on the one hand, and the republicans and Partito d'Azione on the other. The new state saw enemies everywhere: everywhere there were pro-Bourbon elements and Partito d'Azione subversives waiting in ambush. Contemporary reports to the Ministry of the Interior from prefects and sub-prefects frequently show antagonism and suspicion towards local élites. Often new officials seemed to fear the exponents of the Left, who had participated in or supported the expedition of the Thousand and the brief Garibaldian interregnum, more than those nostalgic for the *ancien régime*. Officials, administrators and judges posted to the South found themselves at loggerheads with the local situation, steadfast in their conviction of being representatives of civilization unjustly repulsed. Emblematic of this experience is the case of the trial of the Palermo *'pugnalatori'* (assassins) in 1862—the subject of a story by Sciascia and a study by Pezzino.[13]

The attitude of the exponents of the Historic Right in the South did not mitigate the severity of this judgement; indeed they fully shared the perceptions of the Piedmontese. Having lived for so long in exile and being so deeply influenced by the myths and models of northern Europe, they found themselves out of sympathy with the local situation:

At first absorbed by their studies and then thrown into prison or driven into exile, they had little knowledge of the actual conditions in the country, and furthermore because they had undergone too much suffering, been subjected to too many delusions and too much incomprehension. And now that they had tied their destinies to Italy, they enjoyed the breath of airier climes and felt repugnance at the thought of returning to vulgarity and desperate poverty.[14]

Croce goes on to write that Spaventa, after struggling in 1849 for the salvation of Southern Italy and being, what is more, condemned first to death and then to ten years, imprisonment, preferred to represent a constituency in Northern Italy in the House of Deputies and spoke with irritation of 'that rotten country'.

It was in this period that the theoretical construction of Italian dualism originated. A series of images settled in national public opinion. Photographs of brigands in prison or hanging from the scaffold, and tales of their actual or alleged barbarity, circulated around the country, and lent credibility to the demonic image of the *Mezzogiorno*. This image was soon to receive a further decisive confirmation in the form of positivist racism.

The coming to power of the Left in 1876 marked the entry of the Southern ruling classes into national political life. The nucleus that had led the *Risorgimento* began to dissipate and more broadly based and less homogeneous groupings emerged, with markedly municipalist aspirations. They defended immediate interests, making ample use of local factions to support one party or another. Among those who participated in the *Risorgimento* phase, the disillusionment that was already widespread because of the way Unification had been achieved, now plumbed new depths. At this point a number of Southern intellectuals, who had placed their hopes in intervention from outside and in the adoption of rational models, began criticizing both the government, for its continuing failure to tackle the most serious problems of the South, and Southern society itself, which in their eyes was proving incapable of pursuing modern and dynamic objectives. It was from these reflections that *meridionalismo*—

the body of expertise on the Southern question—began to develop.

The early *meridionalisti*—Pasquale Villari, Giustino Fortunato, Leopoldo Franchetti and Sidney Sonnino—were all positivists and ardent supporters of the unified state. They were above all tireless analysts of the *Mezzogiorno*: they wanted to understand it and make others understand it, without concealment or evasion. They thought that the ruling class of a state which had the extremely difficult task of bringing together such heterogeneous regions had to be in full possession of the facts, so that it could intervene in an equitable and rational manner. Their intention was to combat ignorance about the South and offer a true image in its place. Franchetti and Sonnino declared this openly when they were preparing to depart for Sicily to conduct their inquiry on the *mafia*, and the same spirit inspired Giustino Fortunato's research.

The writings of the *meridionalisti* were mainly based on inquiries carried out in the field. They yielded a body of empirical and sociological information that constitutes the richest collection of social analysis carried out in Italy in the late nineteenth and early twentieth centuries. Of course, it was a positivist myth to believe that once truth emerged from the abyss of ignorance it would be accepted as a matter of course. This myth was to be shattered a thousand times over when it came up against political expediencies. Yet these intellectuals were struggling against some of the most negative features of Italian humanistic culture—unstructured reasoning, the discussion of grand principles without reference to everyday realities, the taking of decisions without knowledge of the relevant facts (see for example Villari, writing in 1875, on the civil service, the army and the reason for its defeat in 1866).[15] They placed the utmost faith in the state's institutions; in the debate over the organization of the civil service they supported a centralist model.

The statist tradition, the idea of the state as the demiurge that intervened to direct society through its reforms, had deep roots in a Southern culture used to confronting centralizing powers (from the Normans to the Bourbons). It was the idea that had inspired the great period of Bourbon public works under the guidance of Afan de Rivera: it consisted, on the one hand, in optimism in a state able to mediate between individuals in the name of the common good, and, on the other, in pessimism—a lack of faith in human nature, in the capacity of the individual to act in the general interest, and, ultimately, a lack of faith in the possibility of self-government,[16] the same lack of faith that Giustino Fortunato expressed in his famous speech in Parliament in 1896 on the question of regionalism.[17] Fortunato was convinced that administrative decentralization would favour the tyranny of factious local power groups:

> It [regionalism] would make the organization of public powers into a vast, ponderous and odious *clientela* ['clientele'] of the dominant classes, and Italy herself an object of luxury at the disposal of whoever has wealth and power, the *signori* ['rulers'] the rich, public officials and politicians.[18]

According to Fortunato, Sonnino and Franchetti, the greatest limitations on the Italian South were on the one hand the poverty and ignorance in which the mass of the people were kept, and which made them incapable of defending themselves and asserting their own interest, and on the other the predatory nature of the ruling classes which further contributed to that poverty and ignorance. This led to the other great battle joined by those who took up the cause of the South: the battle over the social question, which aimed to explain the reasons for the disturbances and rebellions, to open the eyes of those in government to the real condition of the population, and to force them to adopt a more responsible and enlightened attitude. It was an era of considerable social inquiry, to which Pasquale Villari's circle in Florence made a decisive contribution. Naturally they focused on the most dramatic problems: urban poverty, the peasantry working on large estates and *mafia* violence. The images were vividly presented and marked by stark contrasts, for instance between urban poor and élites, peasants and landlords.

The denunciatory tone naturally accentuated the contrasts and obscured the intermediate features. Other factors contributed to the rigid perception of class structure in the South.

The campaign against the protectionist policy for wheat production led people to overestimate the power and the role of the large landowners, and those who knew little about the question were led to think of the South as one vast wheat-growing estate. Moreover, the scientific paradigms of the nineteenth century were unable to grasp the phenomena of social fluidity and mobility. Many of these authors looked to Ricardo and his war on rent in their polemic absentee landlords. In fact, the concepts for grasping and analysing this phenomenon of the middle class with scientific impartiality were inadequate. In addition, the northern European model carried great weight, provoking moralistic judgements. When the members of the professional classes, clerks, and shop-keepers appear, it is only as appendages of the great estates, and they are usually swallowed up in summary descriptions:

> The class of landowners, for lack of any other, became the ruling class, and the municipalities, provinces, charitable bodies, rural police were all in their hands . . . There was no industry, nor bourgeoisie, nor public opinion able to withstand the activities of the landowners who are the absolute lords of that populace which depends on them for its subsistence.[19]

The passage is taken from Villari and was written in 1861, but it would be easy enough to cite hundreds of similar examples from other authors. Many studies have shown how in the nineteenth and twentieth centuries entrepreneurship, social mobility, and the growth of the middle classes had as decisive an effect on the configuration of local élites as on the mass of citizens.[20] The images of the *meridionalisti* in this respect deserve careful reassessment and contextualization. Instead, they have been subjected to the reverse process. Lifted out of the historical context in which they were constructed, such images have been applied to the South as a whole. Moreover, the arguments of these authors that did not fit this framework were systematically set to one side. This then is the traditional conceptual grid that forms the background against which new phenomena that arise are placed. All this contributed to the construction of a rigid and dichotomized image of the social and economic reality of the *Mezzogiorno*.

The idea that Southern society was incapable of self-rule and that the endemic corruption could only be corrected through a powerful initiative from central government is the other great theme that was established by the tradition of nineteenth-century *meridionalismo* and one that has survived to the present. It is interesting to note that a few *meridionalisti* dissented from this view and put forward alternative interpretations and solutions. Napoleone Colajanni, for example, argued that it was precisely the supremacy of the bureaucracy, an uncontrolled and uncontrollable power, that generated corruption. He criticized what he defined as 'fiscal inequality', and claimed it was caused by the state, which 'because of its absurdly centralized organization, acts on the periphery like a suction pump, which only returns a tiny part of what it absorbs'.[21] Gaetano Salvemini, a federalist (a member of the Socialist Party, then after the First World War of the Liberal–Socialist Partito d'Azione) noted for his attacks on the Giolitti government and his savage descriptions of the Southern élites, was convinced that the political control exercised by the prefects over local government and the centralization of the civil service were the fundamental cause of corruption:

> It is not representative government, as Mosca maintains, that produces evils and corruption, but it is representative government coupled with administrative centralization . . . In centralized forms of government the intermediary is necessary not just to pervert the course of justice but to obtain justice pure and simple . . . With federalism money would quit the vicious circle within which it is caught today: money is drawn from all over the place into a single fund, and then it goes out again, but not in the direction of those that have paid but towards those who are most able to take it.[22]

Similar positions were adopted shortly afterwards by Luigi Sturzo (a Sicilian priest and Catholic political activist, founder in 1919 of the Partito Popolare Italiano) and Guido Dorso (like Salvemini, an activist in the Partito d'Azione), but they had little influence on political debate and were destined to be ignored. Even now, such opinions have difficulty in gaining currency in the South.

At the same time that *meridionalismo* was fighting its battle, positivist theories on race were being extensively developed. Alfredo Niceforo, Paolo Orano and others may now seem very distant, but reading them a hundred years on one realizes that their ghosts linger in certain expressions and arguments used today. It has never been sufficiently stressed how profoundly late nineteenth-century racism influenced 'common-sense' social categories and how it continually resurfaces in new forms. Common opinion (and, unfortunately, opinion in some academic circles too) still attributes the same characteristics to Northerners and Southerners as Niceforo, who used the then current terms 'Aryans' (*Ari*) and Mediterraneans. The dark Mediterraneans are individualists, they have very few marked individual characteristics, and consequently their society is 'fragmented' or 'disaggregated'. The peoples of the North, on the other hand, have collective consciousness and therefore social organization, institutions and discipline. Neapolitans, dissolute and weak by nature, are a *popolo donna*, ('a "feminine" people" ') while the others are *'popoli uomini'* (' "masculine" peoples').[23]

In context these statements might appear amusing, but passages of literature, casual conversations, and both popular and academic discussions on the *Mezzogiorno*, in the media emphasize the similarities. I remember a discussion in *La Repubblica* about the fact that in the North people follow the dictates of the father and in the South those of the mother: the male principle and the female principle, very much like Niceforo's male–female distinction. These stereotypes will surface again below in relation to the concept of 'amoral familism'.

Racist positivism had a powerful resonance in the Socialist Party. Its arguments were used to explain, for example, the party's limited success in the South: the causes were not its own political errors but the congenital inability of Southerners to accept the discipline of an organization and their anarchic individualism, which made them disorderly, liable to rebellion and unsuited to long-term political preparation.[24] Filippo Turati, leader of the reformist wing of the Socialist Party, described what he saw as the struggle characterizing Italy:

a struggle between the feudal Middle Ages, which dominates the South and whose tentacles reach out into the entire Italian countryside, and the beginnings of the modern age and industrialization which are dawning in the more civilized and cultured districts, especially in the North. Between these two civilizations, or rather, between an incipient civilization and that putrid barbarity, the battle lines are now drawn. There are two nations in the nation, two Italies in Italy, each one fighting for supremacy.[25]

Salvemini left the Socialist Party because of its widespread anti-Southernism, while Colajanni rebutted one by one the arguments of the racists and the Socialists. It was on the eve of the election at which Crispi, tenacious opponent of the Socialists, was to achieve an important success in Sicily. The Socialists had for some time accused Crispi, their political enemy, of anti-Southern prejudice:

> The bourgeoisie, the real bourgeoisie—the one whose presence and whose development generates socialism and against which Socialism fights . . . has little or nothing in common with the roguery and the brigandage of the oafs and ruffians who have made Crispi their henchman for *mafia* dealings, and who, using every trick in the book, impose themselves on a vast area of the country where the illiterate form 80 per cent of the electorate and the electorate 3 per cent of the living, imposing themselves in turn, with the brute force of numbers, on civilized Italy with disastrous consequences.[26]

Now it was incumbent on them to explain why the popular classes, whom Crispi had humiliated and subjected to a state of siege, should reward him with victory. Colajanni summarizes the coverage in the Socialist press:

> *L'Avanti!* attributes victory to the *mafia* and . . . affirms that moral sense in the South is in short supply. *L'Emancipazione* of Livorno refers to the moral perversion of the vast majority of voters in Palermo. The columnist 'L'uomo di pietra' of Milan in *Risurrezione* (16 April) gives certain rules for voting that are an atrocious insult to the electors of Palermo; in a cartoon entitled 'Southern Tastes', the elector of Palermo wears the traditional

hat of the bandit. *L'Italia del Popolo,* also of Milan, devotes an article to the two moralities—that of the North and that of the South. *La Giustizia* of Reggio Emilia reproduces a shameless pun that Deputy Gabelli once made in the House when he spoke of 'Nordici e Sudici' [trans. 'Northerners and Sweaty Southerners'] . . . when *L'Italia del Popolo* congratulates the citizens and associations of Marsala who had protested against Crispi, it can only do so with reference to 'Sicilians of Northern honesty'.[27]

To summarize, the North voted according to reason, ideals and legitimate interests; the South, by contrast, cast its vote following the dictates of the *mafia*, of favour-seekers and hangers-on and of particularist interests. The South was, in effect, amoral. This case and the comments of the time are strikingly reminiscent of contemporary ones, as are the rebuttals. The arguments used by republicans and Socialists writing about Sicily and the South in general then, are the same as those used to describe the power of certain politicians in the South in more recent times. Why is it that the politicians at the centre of scandal and corruption have enjoyed such unwavering support in the South? Historical events do not seem to offer an explanation, hence the recourse to 'explanations' in terms of an atavistic cultural backwardness—the preference for corruption and a tendency towards irrationalism that bear the mark of original sin, timeless and applicable to the South as a whole. And many of Colajanni's responses would be equally appropriate today. Italians as a whole, said Colajanni, had been apologists of Crispi, more so than the Sicilians. He had gained power due more to national than to local support; the corruption and political methods were ingrained in the centralized system of government of which he was the ultimate exponent. For their part, the Northern Socialists had failed to give support to the Sicilians when they had been engaged in their struggle against the Crispi government (from 1891 to 1893 the Sicilian Fasci had been completely ignored or else treated as a case of barbarous *jacquerie*), but they were then ready to criticize when they voted for Crispi. Finally, Colajanni found parallels to the bloody *mafia* of the South in the activities of white-collar crime of the North, citing examples of corruption—'civilized' crime in the North, 'barbarous' crime in the South.

From 1900 to 1945

A distinctive role in the history of the Southern question was played by Francesco Saverio Nitti, who was of the same generation as Salvemini and Colajanni, and belonged to more or less the same part of the political spectrum, that of radicalism. He was perhaps the figure who most vigorously defended the South's history and interests. His theory was that Italian Unification had been achieved at the South's expense, by squandering its immense financial resources and thus preventing it from developing independently through its own energies.[28] He was convinced that the state had to intervene actively with an industrial policy that would correct the imbalance that had been created. He was the only one of the *meridionalisti* to address the question of industrialization and the only one to hold important government posts.[29]

Around Nitti gathered a group of specialists—engineers, agronomists, financial experts—of considerable standing and of radical Socialist inspiration, many of them Southerners. Together they played a crucial role in government economic policy in the first two decades of the twentieth century. They believed the state had to intervene directly in favour of the industrialization of the South itself, in order to compensate for the tendency in the economy to channel resources and capital towards the North. Technicians and politicians working together with modern industries (notably the electrical industry so important for energy supplies) would have to fight against parasitism and the financial demands of the rent imposed by the great landed estates of the South, the long-time opponents of any type of land reform or improvement. The outcome of their activities include the special legislation for Naples (1904) and for Basilicata (1906–7), the hydro-electric plant at Volturno that provided electricity for the whole of Campania, and the dam at Muro Lucano. However the results are interpreted, this was an impressive attempt, with respect to the *Mezzogiorno* and to Italian politics more generally, to create a ruling group with innovative role for which the slogans were modernity and efficiency combined with pragmatism.

Very little has been said about this group of specialists, and the tradition of *meridionalismo* has not taken up their cause with much vigour. There are many reasons for this, but the distortion and debasement of their ideas and efforts by the Fascists, and later by the Christian Democrats, certainly played a part. The Fascist regime executed some of the land reclamation projects they had devised (specifically for the purpose of generating hydroelectric energy), but instead of using them for a radical transformation of the South's industrial infrastructure, it made them part of its 'ruralization' or 'back to the land' policy, thus depriving the projects of all their revolutionary content.[30] In the period after 1950 their ideas became the symbol of a system of political patronage that made the South even more dramatically dependent on the North than before.

There were, however, some fundamental problems with the theoretical and practical framework devised by the reformers. They were guided by an enlightenment notion, which had already inspired other Southern reformers, that the state could and should act for the good of its subjects, by interpreting progressive reason and imposing it on a blind and unruly population incapable of pursuing its own best interests. Behind this view lay a deep mistrust of the local ruling class, which they believed had to be circumvented. They were unable to identify anyone at local level who could mediate and interpret their plans for innovation. Moreover, such a conception of the ruling class was a long-established element within *meridionalista* thought. In Fortunato's work it was a recurrent theme, representing the dualism that characterized Italy. It was central to Franchetti's considerations on the *mafia*. Perhaps the only lucid critic of this notion was Croce. In a letter of 1911 he affectionately rebuked Fortunato, a good friend of his, for having an excessively pessimistic view of the 'spiritual resources' of the South. Was not he too one part of the picture? Was not he a member of the ruling class against which he pitted himself? In a speech entitled 'The duties of the bourgeoisie' given at a conference in Muro Lucano in memory of a young intellectual killed at the front in 1918, Croce noted that mention was too seldom made of the bourgeoisie and educated groups in the centuries-old struggle against feudalism and in favour of communal rights, while administrations were not always as partisan and ruinous as the polemicists would have us believe.[31]

During this period Dorso, Sturzo and Salvemini were looking at the problem of the ruling classes and Southern pride. Yet deep differences separated them from Croce. Croce refused to regard the *Mezzogiorno* as a specific entity or 'question' and tried, instead, in all his writings to demonstrate the unity that underlay the history of the South with respect to Italian history as a whole.[32] While for Croce the dramatic events that had taken place in the South constituted a necessary part of the difficult process of forming the nation, for Dorso they represented a negative by-product of the enforced dependency of the South and its subjection to the economic system of the North. The 'parasitic oligarchies of the North'[33] had subjugated the Southern ruling classes, dragging them down to the condition of lazy and corrupt agrarian rentiers. Dorso and Salvemini were both convinced that the South could only reassert itself by being autonomous and independent of central government, and that it was the duty of political activists, 'an elite which may be small but which had clear ideas and an unrelentingly critical role', to make sure that the Southern upper and middle classes who were wavering between reaction and progress swung towards the latter. These classes had the extremely important historical task of completing the 'unfinished revolution of the *Risorgimento*' and thus of bringing about a real unification of the country, one that involved the mass of the people. But this could only be achieved after a phase of vigorous assertion of Southern autonomy. In Dorso's words:

> The people of the South need to win self-government, and develop practical solutions which openly reject the requirements of paternalism. If the people of the South finally

understand the need to take their destiny into their own hands
and to abandon the melancholy habit of waiting on Divine
Providence or government charity, this opportunity will not
have been wasted and the lesson of Fascism will have served a
purpose . . . Italy has now existed for seventy years, and no one
is suggesting it should be broken up; its unity has been
considerably reinforced in the recent war, which saw sons of all
its regions fighting and dying side by side . . . But it is precisely
these common services and sacrifices that have given the people
of the South the right to demand the destruction of the old
economic and political order, which the Northern oligarchies
have used to create a veritable dictatorship at the South's
expense, bleeding it dry economically and failing to educate it
politically.[34]

Sturzo had expressed himself in a similar vein in 1901:

Leave us in the South to govern ourselves, plan our own
financial policy, spend our own taxes, take responsibility for our
own public works, and find our own remedies for our
difficulties . . . we are not schoolchildren, we have no need of
the North's concerned protection.[35]

In the years following the First World War—a period of
acute social crisis, when new groups and movements sought
access to power at local and national level—the problem of the
ruling classes became strikingly evident and demanded a more
up-to-date analysis of the class structure. The writings of
Dorso and Sturzo were the first to deal with these issues in a
non-stereotypical way, and they could have led to a more
accurate analysis and a deeper understanding of the social
reality had subsequent events not contributed to the mar-
ginalization of these problems and the prevention of rigorous
scientific analyses. First, the decisive influence of idealist
thought on both right- and left-wing Italian culture (Gramsci
and his influence on the Communists will be discussed below)
was a considerable obstacle to the development of the social
sciences. Then, the Fascist regime contributed not only to
halting political and economic development, but also to the
remodelling of the image of the South on old stereotypes.

Fascism was born in the North, and initially had difficulty

implanting itself in the South, as Dorso pointed out.[36] It was in fact the bloc of Northern moderates who attacked the interventionist policy in the South advocated by Nitti and his followers.[37] As has been noted, land reclamation for the generation of energy and industrialization was transformed into 'land reclamation for ruralization'. During the economic crisis of the late 1920s, as had happened so often before in the history of the South, capital flowed back North, along with control of the economic system. Even the civil service, which after the Italian state's initial 'Piedmontese' phase had been dominated by Southerners, was now 'Northernized', in that the functionaries brought into the state apparatus by the Fascist Party were mainly of Northern origin.[38] The South's dependence on the North increased. Whereas in the North the Fascist regime played a partly modernizing role, at least on the ideological level, in the south its message was populist and ruralist. This produced a very serious setback in the relationship of citizens to public institutions and to the state. Mussolini's populism was particularly influential on the working classes of Naples, whose culture was rooted in the historical memory of the great Bourbon court.[39] Mussolini became the new sovereign–father, unaware of the misdeeds of his subjects, to whom people appealed for justice (this influence continued to be felt after the Second World War, when the people of Naples supported Achille Lauro, a populist and monarchial Fascist, as mayor). Moreover, the new élites also used the Fascist regime to attack the old Liberal élites, justifying their actions in the name of the struggle against patronage and corruption, and depicting Fascism as a system of arbitration and pacification.[40] The idea that only a strong authoritarian state could eradicate corruption and endemic violence became increasingly entrenched.

The period of the Republic: intervention in the South and new stereotypes

After the crushing defeat of the Partito d'Azione in 1947 and the political division of Italy between Catholics and

Communists, regional autonomy and federalism completely disappeared from the debate on the *Mezzogiorno*. Instead Nitti's idea of the state's promotional role was taken up and reinterpreted by the Christian Democrats. Intervention by the Christian Democrat-led governments operated in precisely the manner that had been so fiercely criticized by Sturzo, Dorso and Salvemini, and it exacerbated the South's dependency on central government intervention. Ideological use was made of some of the images of the *meridionalisti*, which were mixed with the modern doctrines of economic backwardness.

The debate started at the end of the 1940s with the theme of backwardness. It was a theme that had already been present in the Enlightenment and in nineteenth-century conceptions of the South, but it was renewed in the theories of development of the 1940s and 1950s. The international political scene had emerged shaken after the Second World War, with traditional colonialist policies in crisis. The problem for the advanced countries was now that of developing international markets by stimulating internal demand through credible development plans. The United States undertook to give considerable financial aid to the war-torn economies of Europe. In Italy the influence of the United States was of considerable importance in the development of state intervention in the South. It operated at a theoretical level through the example of Roosevelt's 'development areas' and in practice through the consultancy of American experts, on loan first to SVIMEZ (Associazione per lo Sviluppo dell'Industria nel Mezzogiorno) and then to the Cassa per il Mezzogiorno.[41] The old images of the South's not keeping pace with the rest of Italy were transferred to the new concept of under-development. Economists and sociologists were brought in to define the economic features of the *Mezzogiorno* (analysed through a series of variables such as income, consumer demand and supply of capital) and measure its distance from the model of growth societies. In other words the debate was about how to trigger development in a society that was considered to be still at zero level. The South was once again a land without history, in a state of nature. This ideology fitted perfectly with the interests of a political leadership—the

Christian Democrats and their allies—whose legitimacy and power were founded on state intervention. The new political class, which identified almost totally with the party of government, the Christian Democrats, returned in some respects to the approach associated with Nitti. However, the proud championing of the historic role of the South was replaced by the request for aid and the assumption of a subordinate role. An élite was forming whose function was that of mediation from a position of dependency involving the syphoning off of resources distributed from the centre. Yet it played this role while simultaneously claiming to interpret and defend a Southern identity. The image of backwardness served as a means of reinterpreting certain aspects of local culture in a thoroughgoing exercise in the 'reinvention of tradition'.[42]

At the same time the response from the Left and Centre was weak. It was limited to the slogan of modernization from above and proved incapable, except during the brief period of the peasant struggles of the late 1940s, of evoking or recreating any form of positive identity. The cultural reference point for the Communist Party was Gramsci's essay of 1926 on the Southern question,[43] which, in stark contrast with the autonomist arguments of Dorso and Salvemini, identified a single way forward in the struggle against a nationally 'unitary' capitalist system, namely a solid alliance between Northern workers and Southern peasantry. In this alliance, however, in line with the Marxist model, it was the working class that was to play the hegemonic role, that of a conscious and modernizing vanguard. For Gramsci, comparing the complicated and uncertain social composition of the South—which he described as *'una grande disgregazione sociale'* ('a great social disintegration')—with the clear class boundaries of Turin, the only possible salvation lay in accepting the solid leadership of the Northern working class.

It is extremely illuminating on this point to look at the controversies in the late 1940s and early 1950s concerning the writings of Ernesto de Martino, Carlo Levi and Rocco Scotellaro.[44] A first debate after the appearance of de Martino's *Il mondo magico* in 1948 was followed by another after the posthumous publication of two books by Scotellaro,[45] the young Socialist mayor of Tricarico in Basilicata. It was Carlo Levi who had discovered and supported Scotellaro, and Levi's *Cristo si è fermato a Eboli* was also brought into this second debate. These authors were all very different from one another: de Martino came to ethnology from the school of Croce and never renounced his debt to the influence and inspiration of the historicist and idealist tradition; Carlo Levi had immersed himself in the Southern peasant culture as a political internee in a small village in Lucania during the Fascist period and had developed a sympathetic or (in his words) 'inner' understanding of that world. Rocco Scotellaro, a young Socialist mayor in Lucania, used to write poetry and explore the local culture. Through Levi, he went to work at the research centre in Portici under Manlio Rossi-Doria and began a major project on popular culture in the *Mezzogiorno*, collecting biographies and interviews from peasants. He died prematurely and it was Levi and Rossi-Doria who edited his work after his death, but what they had in common was the desire to interpret the popular culture of the South. Their books raise complex problems which cannot be explored adequately here. The idea of the peasant world as an enclosed and uniform whole is not convincing; nor is the way the peasant from Basilicata or Calabria is made into a symbol of the human condition of pain and oppression, which almost becomes a universal category in the case of de Martino, who examines superstition and magic in relation to an argument about the crisis of reason. These were, however, important attempts to understand a culture from within, to restore a measure of dignity to it, and to explore what would nowadays be called its intrinsic rationality.

Their critics, however, challenged the legitimacy of the whole operation, flatly rejecting any possibility of saving a world they considered an anachronistic relic and an obstacle to the reawakening of the Southern masses. They argued therefore—and on this point Crocean idealists and Marxist historicists were in agreement—that it was a world that had to be rejected totally. It is astonishing to read today the arguments used by critics of the time who accused de Martino, Scotellaro and Levi of irrationalism,[46] of populism (because they had not 'sufficiently acknowledged the special role of the working class' and its vanguard function in relation to the Southern masses,[47] of appealing to the popular and the primitive,[48] and of diverting the Southern masses from their alliance with the working class.[49] The irrelevancy of the whole debate drove the authors, in order that they might defend themselves from the accusations of obscurantism and conservatism, to seek explanations and propose solutions that were not always in line with their own analyses. In the end their true message was obscured, their images were recovered within the ideology of backwardness, put on one side and used to describe an archaic world that needed to be superseded. They thus had the effect of confirming one of the many stereotypes about the *Mezzogiorno*: that of its immobility and its exclusion from history.

Shortly afterwards, Edward Banfield's work on 'amoral familism' arrived in Italy from the United States. The concept was used by Banfield to explain the principal characteristic of the society he studied, a poor and isolated village in Basilicata, where he lived with his family for a year. He also proposed it as a more general analytical category through which to interpret the causes of Southern Italy's backwardness as a whole. *The Moral Basis of a Backward Society* appeared in English in 1958,[50] and was translated into Italian in 1961. It made an important contribution to the cultural debate of the 1960s on the question of backwardness and its causes, and like other studies of the period it attempted to respond to the questions posed by Third World aid policies. Banfield, an anthropologist and political scientist, asked what mechanisms existed for allocating and redistributing resources and power in societies dominated by scarcity, and whether the values attached to these mechanisms were an obstacle to development and modernization. A study that parallels that of Banfield is G.M. Foster's work on a Mexican community.[51] The societies represented by the two authors embody two extremes in the confrontation of the problem of scarcity. On the one hand, there is 'amoral familism'—the total and unregulated competition involving individuals whose only objective is the welfare of their own children. On the other, the Mexican case displays rigid community controls over economic exchanges and mechanisms of accumulation that entail a mythical egalitarianism designed to prevent the formation of surpluses and severely limit social differentiation and mobility. The term 'amoral familism' describes a form of behaviour directed solely towards the pursuit of the good of the family, understood here in the more restricted sense of parents and children. It implies therefore an endemic inability to act in the common good—what is popularly called a lack of civic consciousness. It is related to societies where the fundamental unit is the nuclear family and more complex forms of social organization are absent. It is often associated with centralized and authoritarian states, which discourage growth of intermediate institutions of government between the state and its citizens. Its original causes include poverty, authoritarianism in social relations and, above all, the absence of the extended patriarchal family, a complex organization capable of producing and disseminating throughout society organizational ability, a sense of collective duty and the practice of co-operation and solidarity. Such was the picture drawn by Banfield and such were his categories, which produced a heated debate when his book appeared. The controversy had little influence on the studies of *meridionalisti* in the years that followed. In the 1960s and 1970s they deliberately ignored questions of culture and values. It did, however, have an effect on perceptions of the South in the form of public opinion.

It is valuable to retrace the chain of reasoning that led the paradigm of amoral familism to become so firmly established, because it provides a close-range view of how a stereotype is constructed. Amoral familism was stripped of its descriptive and scientific content, and it became used to mean simply the tendency of Southerners to favour the family group; as such it was identified as one of the major causes of clientelism or patronage. In this way, the strength of the family was linked to the persistence of tradition, and tradition, in its turn, was linked to the extended patriarchial and patrilinear family, dominated by the ties of blood. This view was partly the natural effect of a simplistic idea of how family groups developed in the West, an idea which has held sway over sociological and historical analyses for a long time, and has been propagated through the mass media, taking root at all levels of society. This is the idea that in 'traditional' peasant societies the extended and patriarchal family is predominant, and that with the transition to so-called modernity the family becomes nuclear, kinship ties slacken and choices become individualized. Thus, in this reworking of Banfield's concept, Southern society, already considered 'backward' and 'traditional' according to one powerful stereotype, now also becomes patriarchal. Hence Banfield's argument was unwittingly turned on its head, the prevalence of the patriarchal family was identified as the reason for the strength of kinship and its pervasiveness in the social and political fabric and the category of amoral familism was misused. The experts in the field are practically the only ones who avoid this confusion.

At the same time, this stereotyped perception has coincided with another, which is closer to Banfield's original idea: that of a fragmented South, lacking valid principles of social organization, dominated by extreme individualism, riven by the war of all against all, incapable of creating permanent group identities—the South of the *mafia* and competition over limited resources. This image is all the more tenacious because it has been superimposed on older perceptions: consider the statement by Niceforo quoted above. Thus there is a principle of order (the patriarchal and hierachical family typified by subordination of its members to the group strategy) and a principle of fragmentation and disorder. Apparently the contradiction between these two images is ignored.

The history of the concept of amoral familism illustrates well the processes by which the image of the Mezzogiorno has been constructed. Both within the South and outside it, the image of backwardness has been adopted. Empirical data have been inserted into this framework, and if they have not fitted they have been adapted, reinterpreted or ignored. An identical phenomenon, the patriarchal family—commonly associated with underdevelopment—goes unnoticed if it relates to a society in the North, whereas it is immediately considered and presented as part of an integrated perspective if it relates to the South. Thus, the representations of patriarchal families in the

Veneto or Tuscany are neutral facts not worthy of mention, while similar images referring to the South make a powerful impression on public opinion, confirm the mental model and guarantee its perpetuation.

These images are constructed within the North–South dialogue, but Southerners are the first to believe them and appropriate them. In the past I have examined students of contemporary history at the University of Naples on a text that among other things dealt with the family in European history. I tried many times to ask students what type of family they thought was prevalent in Southern society, and they all replied: the patriarchal family. Anyone who has observed and studied Southern society impartially knows very well that the patriarchal family practically does not exist there (if one excludes bourgeois and aristocratic families of the nineteenth and early twentieth centuries, which were in any case patriarchal throughout Europe at that time). They would also know that women have a 'traditional' power there which is unquestionably greater than that of other Italian women— division of wealth between the sexes according to an equitable method, careful protection of the dowry throughout a woman's life and its direct inheritance by her children, enormous moral and contractual power within the family, and so forth. But the everyday image is filtered or even obscured by a conviction rooted in the nature of common opinion. This opinion is confirmed by interactions with a North that is admired and turned into a myth.

When we interpret something 'unknown', we do so by inserting it into the system of meanings of a culture accumulated in a specific historical context and in the course of our own life. Often we select only the information that fits into our pre-established image. In this way, the representation is reinforced in a vicious circle, it becomes a reality inasmuch as the person who is its object accepts it, and, if he or she is weaker, ends up taking it on and identifying with it. I have often heard things which I experienced as a girl in a large Northern city described as examples of the startling conditions in which women live in the South: sexual taboos, the difficulties of communication between generations, the impossibility of going out in the evening, fear of one's neighbours. These features were probably common to the whole of Italy in a specific generation, but when they are combined with the term *Mezzogiorno* they take on a very different meaning and manage to convince Southerners, who cannot easily make comparisons, that they are living in a unique situation of centuries-old inferiority. Interaction does not automatically mean understanding, as can be seen from the terrifying ethnic conflicts which are devastating part of eastern Europe. From this point of view, the faith the advocates of *meridionalismo* placed in a peaceful osmosis between cultures based on mutual knowledge has proved to be a great illusion—an illusion that is still deeply rooted in common-sense opinion.

It is worth reflecting on the amazed reaction to events in the former Yugoslavia. Is it possible, it was asked, that people who have lived together for centuries are now fighting one another in the name of ethnic difference? And how can they appeal to images, symbols and prejudices based on events that took place hundreds of years ago? It is a commonplace assumption that everyday interaction leads to hybridization of cultures, a melting pot, and to the creating of reciprocal tolerance in the place of cultural and ethnic frontiers. The very same set of assumptions underpinned the nineteenth-century project of Unification and the rejection of any kind of federalism, namely that contact between Italians, through military service in a different region and exposure to identical political and institutional structures, would bring about peaceful integration and, above all, the assimilation of the South by the culture of the North. It is a positivist vision in which interaction means exchange of information and ever closer approximation to the truth. Truth, in this perspective, dispels suspicion and drives out prejudice. Territorial borders like ethnic divisions are cultural first and foremost, even if they are more powerful when linked with material interests or when they are mobilized in the struggle for leadership within a state.

Although the conflict between North and South in Italy has not ended in bloodshed, it is developing in a similar manner to that in eastern Europe. The integration between the two areas is very considerable: one need only consider all the inter-marriages between Northerners and Southerners, the assimilation into the Northern cities of the Southern migrants of the 1950s and 1960s, the high number of Southerners amongst the Italian ruling class, not only in the ranks of the discredited state bureaucracy (in Milan, for example, there is a substantial group of company directors who were born in Naples and graduated there before migrating northwards). Despite all this, there is currently a marked return to the divisive arguments of the nineteenth century, but with even greater malice. Integration has not diminished the negative stereotype. This new situation has been brought about by political events, vested interests and problems of national leadership, and the North–South cultural categorization has provided an ideal vehicle for rekindling conflicts and channelling hatreds. The image of the South has entered a vicious circle in which it is increasingly stereotyped.

NOTES

1. L. Cafagna, *Nord e Sud* (Venice, 1994).
2. G. Simmel, *Über soziale Differenzierung* (Berlin, 1890); G. Simmell, *Soziologie* (Berlin, 1908); R.K. Merton, *Social Theory and Social Structure* (New York, 1949).
3. P. Bourdieu, *Distinction. A Social Critique of the Judgement of Taste*, trans. R. Nice (London, 1984).
4. Y.M. Lotman, *Universe of the Mind: A Semiotic Theory of Culture*, trans. A. Shukman (London, 1990).
5. J. Agnew, 'Italia arretrate, Europa moderna', *Il Mulino*, 351 (1994).
6. F. Fucini, *Napoli a occhio nudo* (Turin, 1976); see also on Naples, J. White-Mario, *La miseria di Napoli* (Florence, 1877).
7. B. Croce, *Storia del Regno di Napoli* (Milan, 1992), 335–360.
8. See A. Mozzillo, *Viaggiatori stranieri nel Sud* (Milan, 1984); A. Mozzillo, *Viaggi e viaggiatori nel Mezzogiorno borbonico* (Naples, 1992).
9. C. Levi, *Cristo si è fermato a Eboli* (Turin, 1945); F. Frenaye, trans. *Christ stopped at Eboli* (London, 1967).
10. L. Sterne, *Sentimental Journey* (London, 1994); J.W. Goethe, *The Italian Journey* trans. W.H. Auden and E. Mayer (London, 1962); (London, 1962).
11. A. Mozzillo, *Viaggi*, 24.
12. N. Moe, 'Il Sud dei piemontesi (1860–61)', *Meridiana*, 15, (1992).
13. L. Sciascia, *I pugnalatori* (Turin, 1976); P. Pezzino, *La congiura dei pugnalatori* Venice, 1992).
14. B. Croce, *Storia del regno di Napoli*, 349.
15. P. Villari, *Le lettere meridionali*, (Naples, 1979).

16. C. d'Elia, *Bonifiche e stato nel Mezzogiorno, 1815–60* (Naples, 1994).
17. G. Fortunato, *Carteggio, 1865–1911* (Bari, 1978).
18. G. Fortunato, *Il mezzogiorno e lo stato italiano* (Bari, 1911).
19. P. Villari, *Le lettere meridionali*, 69, 73.
20. See B. Salvemini, 'Note sul concetto di Ottocento meriodionale', *Società e Storia*, 26 (1984); B. Salvemini, 'Prima della Puglia', *Storia d'Italia: Le regioni dall'Unità a oggi, La Puglia*, (Turin, 1989); P. Frascani, 'Mercato e commercio a Napoli dopo l'Unità', in *Storia d'Italia: Le regioni dall'Unità a oggi, La Campania* (Turin, 1990); G. Gribaudi, *A Eboli. Il mondo meridionale in cent'anni di trasformazione* (Venice, 1990); S. Lupo, *Il giardino degli aranci. Il mondo degli agrumi nella storia del Mezzogiorno* (Venice, 1990).
21. N. Colajanni, *In Sicilia* (Rome, 1894), 42.
22. G. Salvemini, *Scritti sulla questione meridionale* (Turin, 1955), 110–19.
23. A. Niceforo, *L'Italia barbara contemporanea* (Milan–Palermo, 1998) 293.
24. A. Niceforo, *Italiani del Nord e Italiani del Sud* (Turin, 1901).
25. F. Turati, 'Tattica elettorale', *La critica sociale* (Milan, 1895), 79.
26. 'Saprofiti politici', *La critica sociale*, (1895), 13, 193–96; cited in A. Asor Rosa, 'La cultura', *Storia d'Italia, IV*, 2, (Turin, 1975).
27. N. Colajanni, *Settentrionale e Meridionale* (Milan–Rome, 1898).
28. F.S. Nitti, *Scritti sulla questione meridionale* (Bari, 1958).
29. F. Barbagallo, *Francesco Saverio Nitti* (Turin, 1984).
30. G. Barone, *Mezzogiorno e modernizzazione* (Turin, 1986).
31. B. Croce, *Il dovere della borghesia nelle province napoletane* (Bari, 1924).
32. G. Galasso, *Croce, Gramsci ed altri scritti* (Milan, 1969).
33. G. Dorso, *La rivoluzione meriodionale* (Turin, 1924), 217.
34. Ibid, 216–18.
35. L. Sturzo, 'La questione del Mezzogiorno', *La croce di Costantino*, ed., G. de Rosa (Rome, 1958).
36. G. Dorso, *La rivoluzione meridionale*, ch. 6.
37. G. Barone, *Mezzogiorno*.
38. M. Salvati, *Il regime e gli impiegati* (Rome–Bari, 1992).
39. P. Varvaro, *Una città fascista. Potere e società a Napoli* (Palermo, 1990).
40. G. Gribaudi, *A Eboli*.
41. G. Gribaudi, *Mediatori. Aatropologia del potere democristiano nel mezzogiorno* (Turin, 1980); S. Cafiero, *Tradizione e attualità nel meridionalismo* (Bologna, 1987).
42. G. Gribaudi, *Mediatori*; G. Gribaudi, *A Eboli*.
43. A. Gramsci, 'Alcuni temi della questione meridionale (1926)', *La construzione del Partito Comunista* (Turin, 1971).
44. P. Clemente, M.L. Meoni and M. Squillacciotti, *Il dibattito sul folklore in Italia*, (Milan, 1976); P. Angelini, ed., *Dibattito sulla cultura delle classi subalterne* (Rome, 1977).
45. R. Scotellaro, *Contadini del Sud* (Bari, 1954); R. Scotellaro, *È fatto giorno* (Milan, 1954).
46. B. Croce, 'Intorno al magismo come età storica', *Filosofia e storiografia* (Turin, 1949).
47. C. Luporini, 'Intorno alla storia del mondo popolare subalterno', *Società*, 1 (1950).

48. F. Fortini, 'Il diavolo sa trasvestirsi da primitivo', *Paese Sera*, (23 February 1950).

49. M. Alicata, 'Il meridionalismo non si può fermare a Eboli', *Cronache meridionali*, 9 (1954).

50. E. Banfield, *The Moral Basis of a Backward Society* (Glencoe, 1958).

51. G.M. Foster, *Tzin Tzun Tzan. Mexican Peasants in a Changing World* (Boston, 1967).

6

Stereotypes of the Italian South 1860–1900

JOHN DICKIE

Introduction

One does not have to spend long in Italy to discover not only how frequent are incidents of intolerance towards Southerners, but also how sensitive Italian public culture is to that intolerance. One does not have to read into Italian history very far to discover similar moments of intolerance and sensitivity. My work is an inquiry into how one can write the history of these moments and the anxieties they betray, into how one can describe the specific cultural and social texture and import-ance of ethnocentric stereotypes of the South in different contexts. At present my study is limited to the years between Unification and the end of the nineteenth century, when the governing élite was united in a single state, but when new social forces had not begun to find substantial representation in that state. It is that social context, I believe, which deter-mines the range of meanings bestowed on stereotypical representations of the South.

The concepts of 'prejudice', 'intolerance', 'racism' and 'ethnocentrism' (my own preference is for the last of these) are problematic and controversial. I therefore make no apologies for beginning with some theory, even if there is no space here for the full definition of my terms which the question demands. The *locus classicus* of prejudice towards Southern

Italians is Alfredo Niceforo's *L'Italia barbara contemporanea (Contemporary Barbarian Italy)* of 1898. By way of introduction, I want to use some aspects of *L'Italia barbara contemporanea*, a text often invoked and yet rarely analysed, to bring into relief the problem of ethnocentrism towards the South, especially as concerns the notion of 'regionalism' which I think has tended to obscure the real significance of that ethnocentrism. I want to use Niceforo to demonstrate the need to relocate the narrow issue of prejudice towards the South in the broader and more complex question of the status attributed to images of the South in the whole culture.

Niceforo argues that Sicily, Sardinia and the Southern mainland are stagnating at an inferior level of social evolution to the northern and central provinces. The South is feudal, semi-civilized and even barbaric: 'Sardinia, Sicily and the *Mezzogiorno* are three peoples who are still primitive, not completely evolved, less civilized and refined than the populations of the North and Centre of Italy.'[1]

Niceforo's portrait of the 'collective psyche' of the population of the South is based on the favoured criteria by which positivist sociology is measured on the state of civilization of a people: crime, education, birth rate, mortality, suicide rate and the economy. But craniometric data is also used to argue that the difference between North and South is racial and that race is the root cause of the greater individualism of the South and superior sense of social organization of the North. Niceforo concludes that Italy's hopes for the future rest on its becoming a federal state, since specific forms of government are necessary to deal with the distinct characteristics of each region: government must be authoritarian in the South and liberal in the North.

Prejudice towards the South is frequently attributed to regionalism. The assumption is that enmity between different regions and between the regions and the central state stem directly from the real economic and social diversity of Italy's provinces. Both Antonio Gramsci and Massimo Salvadori, in his classic history of the Southern question *Il mito del buongoverno*, regard social anthropologists like Niceforo as having sown discord between the two halves of Italy: in the

Quaderni, the debate over Niceforo is called 'a North–South polemic on races and on the superiority and inferiority of the North and the South'.[2] Yet if the racial thesis provoked a polemic between North and South as Gramsci maintains, and if, as Salvadori asserts, the socio-biological understanding of the Southern question was simply a 'work of defamation' against southerners,[3] then it is difficult to account for the fact that its central text was written by a Sicilian: Niceforo refers to 'my soul born at the foot of Etna' in the introduction to *L'Italia barbara contemporanea*.[4] Even in the case of what Salvadori regards as the *ne plus ultra* of hatred towards the South, ethnic prejudices do not necessarily pit the inhabitants of the two halves of Italy against each other in a clear-cut way. To attribute texts such as *L'Italia barbara contemporanea* to inter-regional prejudice is to leave unexplained not just the question of how regional belonging might work, but indeed the very idea of a region. The task presented to the historian by anti-Southern ethnocentrism is therefore not a biographical one, and not, in the initial stages, a socio-historical one, but one of textual interpretation: it is not to trace how Sicily or Sicilian society influenced Niceforo, for example, but to study what concepts such as 'Sicily' mean in his text.

My referring to Sicily as a concept begs further explanation. Writers on the Southern question have frequently pointed out that the diversities within both North and South are as great as those between them. The South, moreover, is at different times taken to mean 'South and islands' and 'mainland South'. It sometimes includes Rome and sometimes stops below it. But rather than attempt to resolve the terminological or geo-graphical imprecision in the definition of North and South, I suggest that one must try to explain the insistent presence of that imprecision. Edward Said's *Orientalism* offers a theoretical model for such an explanation. Said writes the history of the Orient, that vague geographical definition, which has been taken to have some sort of explanatory force in relation to the vastly different realities of the Middle East, the Indian subcontinent and the Far East. The South, like the Orient, is a construct; in Said's words, it is 'a constituted entity'.[5] The notion of 'the South' may have a greater utility in certain contexts than does 'the Orient' (it certainly pretends to embrace a diversity less preposterously vast). Nevertheless, as soon as the thought 'the South' occurs it becomes an area of political intervention, the place with a history or a characteristic political culture, the object of loyalties, the bearer of certain psychological traits, the sum or average of the diverse social realities within it, it becomes a concept. For Niceforo, for example, all of the varied aspects of his account of the *Mezzogiorno*—statistical, anecdotal, sociological, behavioural, racial, historical—are interrelated because he conceives of the South in a particular way, as 'an organic whole'.[6] If, in a study of representations, we try a priori to define the South, and thereby assume that it is a social or cultural given, we risk repeating that kind of reification. By adopting this approach I do not intend to suggest that one cannot differentiate between good and bad uses of 'the South'. I want rather to build into my readings an awareness of the fact that the South does not cease to be a concept when it is used well: to write of the South is always a discursive operation which is susceptible to textual forces which can become historically invisible to the reader whose priority is to determine the greater or lesser degree of referential accuracy of the text concerned. My work is therefore a study of how the concept of the South is formed in certain texts of the post-Unification period, not as the reflection, refraction or occlusion of a reality, but as the effect of operations of discourse which themselves are implicated in the social realities of the period. I aim not to demonstrate the falsity of perceptions of the South by comparison with a world which they have distorted, but to treat those perceptions as an object of study in their own right.

A further danger related to an undertheorized notion of regionalism is that of isolating a text like *L'Italia barbara contemporanea* from its national frame of reference. It is undoubtedly true that Niceforo's text was seen to speak to the mood of hostility towards Rome and the South in the Milan of the 1890s. Strong regionalist movements like those in Milan did indeed compete with and feed off the centralizing tendencies of the state and often produced their own brand of bigotry.[7] But Niceforo's ethnocentrism was essentially of an

incorporative rather than an exclusive kind. Although he was a
federalist, Niceforo did not want to divided North from South,
but to create a more flexible and therefore a stronger unity
between them. He thus felt able to align himself with a
tradition of patriotic social thinkers on the Southern question.
He firmly believed that, although racially different,
Northerners and Southerners were as one in their 'spirit of
nationality'.[8] Throughout *L'Italia barbara contemporanea* and
the debate that followed, Niceforo and others saw their work
on Southern Italy as the victory of science over two opposing
taboos :a short-sighted regional pride on the part of those who
refused to consider the problems of other areas of the country;
and a cult of national unity, which sought dogmatically to fit all
of Italy's diverse regions into one administrative model.
Niceforo's book is also a response to the crisis of colonial
expectations after the calamitous defeat of Italian troops by a
native arm at Adowa in 1896. Referring to the South, Niceforo
says in his introduction: 'Here modern Italy has a lofty mission
to accomplish and a great colony to civilize.'[9] Niceforo writes
not as a Southerner or as a Northerner, but as an Italian. The
problems he speaks about are considered Italian problems. The
agent to be responsible for their solution is Italy. The worrying
thing about *L'Italia barbara contemporanea*, as with many other
texts about the South, is not their excessive provincialism, but
the particular form of their nationalism. Therefore, what I offer
here is *not* an interpretation of Northern perceptions of the
South. It is rather a reading of images of the South from many
sources, both Northern and Southern, and against the background of attempts to create or imagine a nation.

What, then, were the relations between images of the South
and the nation? Representations of the *Mezzogiorno* from the
centres of political and cultural power in Liberal Italy were
often constructed from a repertoire of stock scenes and
images. *L'Italia barbara contemporanea* is almost an inventory of
the stereotypes of the South in the late nineteenth century: the
mafia and *camorra*; the lottery, brigandage and feudalism;
illiteracy, superstition and magic; cannibalism and corruption;
Southerners as 'woman-people', yet whose society is based on
an 'Arabic' oppression of women; Southerners as patho-

logically individualistic, yet indistinguishable in their teeming masses; dirt and disease as characteristic of the *Mezzogiorno* together with rustic beauty. The common element in such stereotypes was the construction of the South as an Other to Italy and to totemic values considered all but synonymous with it. In straightforward terms, to define Italy as civilized, one has to have a sense, albeit perhaps implicit, of where that civilization fades at its boundaries into the barbarous. The South was one Italy's most important banks of images of Otherness. The barbarous, the primitive, the violent, the irrational, the feminine, the African: these an other values, negatively connoted, were repeatedly located in the *Mezzogiorno* as foils to definitions of Italy.

My work is based on a particular understanding of the nation. Anthony Giddens has described nationalism as 'the cultural sensibility of sovereignty',[10] as the way we think and feel our relationship to the state. Whatever manifestations of nationalism may not be covered by this pithy definition, it does seem to capture one of its most important and complex functions. The nation is one of the legitimating premises of a vast and complex form of social organization. Yet the most minute routines and traditions through which citizenship is acted out can in the right circumstances become connotative of nationhood: from saluting a flag to carrying out a financial transaction, from looking at a book, building or landscape to uttering a stereotype. Nations, as Benedict Anderson has argued, have to be imagined.[11] The emotional and intellectual grip of nationalism is due in part to an imaginary topography: to feel part of a nation, one has to be able to imagine its extent and be sensitive to its symbolic frontiers. Nationalism involves the constant renegotiation of conceptions of the individual and the wider social world: to be a citizen is to have learnt how to use and respond to the language of nationality. Nationalism is thus indispensable to the state, and yet it has the fragility of conceptual thought: its great power may ultimately only depend on the textually precarious differentiation of friend and foe, Self and Other. That combination of social importance and conceptual contingency makes the language of nationhood one of the most sensitive indicators of conflict and unease in a society like post-*Risorgimento* Italy and around a problem like the *Mezzogiorno*.

Yet nationalism, at least when understood as something like 'the cultural sensibility of sovereignty', can only have been irrelevant to the vast, 'un-Italianized majority in post-Unification Italy. Even Niceforo was too optimistic in his belief that the country was held together 'by the bond of national awareness'.[12] But to call that majority 'Italians' is not wholly anachronistic; it is, as Raffaele Romanelli and others have pointed out, consonant with the terms of reference of the country's governing class.[13] Indeed, the creaking conceptual apparatus organized around the name of 'Italy' was a component of the mentality of all of the social groups who were represented in the institutions. Among those groups were many Southerners, often thought to include the strongest believers in the unified, central state. The state was the fragile cement of Italy's ruling bloc, and the ideology which signified allegiance to it, the language in which its affairs were conducted, was patriotism. If the Italian state had few interlocutors outside of its institutions, its dialogue with those within them, if it was far from open and harmonious, was certainly intense. Moreover, the distance which separated the Italian élites and their state from the masses was not only a material divide: it was also an issue of perceptions and imaginings. An insistent concern about the classes beyond the institutions was often thought of in the terms provided by nationality, as a question of 'making Italians'. What I want to argue is that stereotypes of the South can be read in the context of those terms and that concern. I aim to tease out the ambivalent and ambiguous meanings of 'Italy', the 'Italian people' and associated notions which are involved in different representations of the South.

My approach demands an attention to the textual and contextual detail which determines the meaning and force of representations of the South. I have accordingly produced four individual analyses which are intended to illustrate the diversity, tenacity and complexity of ethnocentric representations of the South: the first deals with the Italian army's campaign against brigandage in the South after 1860; the second with

Pasquale Villari's posing of the Southern question; the third with representations of the South in the *Illustrazione Italiana*; the last with the public image of Francesco Crispi. In the short space available here I can only hope to sample the complex issue of imaginary constructions of the South, and perhaps, in doing so, to generate a wider interest.[14]

The anti-brigandage campaign, 1860–70

The bloody and protracted war fought by the Italian army against so-called brigandage in the years after 1860 was the first traumatic encounter between the new state and the South. What the representatives of the state encountered in the South was not only some thorny social and political realities but also some of their own worst cultural nightmares. My own interest in the war centres on the functions of the concept of brigandage in the Italian army's campaign. The ways in which brigandage and the South were imagined played a role in the tactically important discourses through which the officer class understood their enemy and what they perceived to be their nation-building role. The war was also the occasion for fears and fantasies which, as we shall see, fed into the interpretation and enactment of rules and orders. But since some of my work on brigandage is already in the public domain, I thought it best here to give only a brief summary of my case and then to concentrate on one particular incident, which illustrates some of my points.[15]

There was no single reality of brigandage; no one group of people or type of activity matches the label 'brigands' or 'brigandage'. Brigandage was a cluster of events, relations and perceptions produced and acted out by the different agents involved in the campaign. The Italian army's definitions of banditry tell us as much about their tactics, but also their fears and uncertainties, as about the reality of their enemy. For the army, brigandage functioned as a conceptual grid through which a great variety of activities were understood. Aspects of the war as diverse as legal debates and executions by firing squad were informed by particular conceptualizations of banditry, which, despite a great variety of explanations of the causes and nature of the conflict, had two insistent characteristics. Of these, the first was an anathematization of brigandage as the inversion of the nation, society or the law; in the minds of the officer class, and of sections of Northern Italian society, the fight against banditry became the battle between civilization and barbarism, reason and violence, humanity and inhumanity, social order and crime. Animality, to give just one example, is a constant theme of writers on brigandage: 'They kill and rape like beasts thirsty for blood and booty and not men created in the image of God.'[16] The second feature was a persistent vagueness about what brigandage actually was, a constant resorting to metaphors to describe what a member of the parliamentary commission set up to inquire into the problem called the 'funereal mystery' of banditry.[17] This vagueness extended even to circulars from the authorities to the commanders in the field: 'The crime of brigandage . . . is a continuous crime which has an indeterminate character which includes all those crimes and felonies committed by those who go about ravaging the countryside for this purpose in numbers of three or more.'[18]

Conceptualizations of brigandage are set in the broader frame of an imaginative geography in which the South is constructed as an alien land, like Africa or the Orient. Nino Bixio, writing to his wife while working with the parliamentary commission of inquiry into brigandage, exclaims, '. . . this in short is a country which ought to be destroyed or at least depopulated and its inhabitants sent to Africa to get themselves civilized!'[19]

One of Cavour's envoys in the South in 1860 wrote: 'What barbarism! Some Italy! This is Africa: the beduoin are the flower of civilized virtues compared to these peasants.'[20]

In May 1865, near Potenza, Vito Francolino was condemned to death. Like many captured brigands he was to be shot in the back to symbolize his unworthiness even for the conventional military execution. (Extreme offences such as raping children and betraying the army to an enemy were the only ones normally punished in this way.) However, on hearing the order to fire, Francolino ducked, and, although wounded, made off across the countryside pursued by the firing party, who sustained a number of injuries before the fugitive was captured and bayonetted on the spot. The case drew the attention of the minister of war, concerned about the conduct of Captain Bertagni, who had been in charge. The commander of the local military tribunal wrote to the ministry about the case. More than Bertagni's incompetence in letting Francolino escape, it was the irregularity of the brigand's death which provoked the 'indignation' of the commander:

> Far more than for the lack of the necessary precautions, Captain Bertagni ought to answer for the subsequent inhuman killing of the fugitive, an incident which dishonours the army . . . The brigand Francolino had been condemned to be shot and not to be barbarically slaughtered with sword and bayonet blows.[21]

The key words here are 'inhuman' and 'barbarically'. These terms were habitually, one might even say automatically, applied to brigands and their activities. But here they are used against Captain Bertagni, and suggest that Francolino should expect, even in death, treatment befitting his humanity, a humanity normally denied to brigands. The letter is one of many instances where the terms in the polarities through which the army constructed the notion of brigandage were reversed; they are articulate self-doubt as well as aggression.

The letter goes on to imply that the misapplied death penalty had already served a moralizing, humanizing purpose for the victim whose actual death would no longer have been required. Francolino's escape is taken as evidence of his residual humanity, and should have been the occasion for a patriotically connoted magnanimity to be applied: 'Francolino was no longer at that point a brigand but a patient, who had already suffered the spasms of his final agony. Sentiments of humanity and the generous pride of the Italian Soldier spoke eloquently in his favour . . .'[22]

An important factor in the commander's concern about the case is the bad publicity which would accrue to the army. While operating in the public eye as a representative of the Italian nation, the military had also to respond to the desires of its audience, whose hearts and minds were, after all, the stake in the war. The letter mentions that if the escapee had been recaptured alive, a second shooting would probably not have been ordered, 'it being precisely one of the cases in which Royal mercy would have been opportune and would have met with the unanimous plaudits of those people.'[23] Administering justice to a brigand was something of a spectacle. Executions were often carried out in town squares. Failing that, the corpses or heads of bandits could be put on public display. But this theatre of justice was very much at odds with the normal military judicial practice focused on dealing with the individual wrongdoer and operating not in dialogue with a public but according to an ethos of systematic impartiality. The idea, which crystallized almost to the point of becoming official policy, was that by watching a powerful judicial and military apparatus in operation, Southerners would have instilled in them a sense of legality which they had lost. Old stereotypes of the 'impressionable' Southern character were revived to legitimate such tactics. The following quotations are from the correspondence between General La Marmora and Prime Minister Ricasoli: 'To Southern peoples one must give the example of a strong government and impartial administration . . . Your Excellency knows only too well how this population is impressionable: to believe it has to be able to see.'[24]

If areas of the South were conceived of as being outside the nation and the law during the anti-brigand campaign, as being an Africa or an Orient, this was not because the army sought consciously and unscrupulously to legitimate the unchecked use of brutal repression. Indeed, the Southern population were often see as being outside the law as naïve spectators: the forces of order had therefore to work no longer by impartiality in individual cases, but by putting themselves on display, by staging a daily judicial melodrama.

In a latter communication to the War Ministry on the case of Francolino, the status of the brigand is distinctly different: 'I thought, and I still think that an officer who soils his sword in the blood of someone condemned to death is no longer fit to wear it.'[25] Here it is as if the officer's 'inhumanity' is contracted by a form of contamination from the criminal's taboo-laden body. The hygienic, impersonal distance which the regulations prescribe between executor and victim, law and criminal, has been closed. The metaphors of dirt which apply to the brigand here are the reverse of the humanitarian rhetoric quoted above: the 'barbaric' brigand figure seems here to be making a return.

What this one incident demonstrates is the kind of legal and conceptual confusion engendered in the army by the war against brigandage: the Manichaean certainties of the national battle against an uncivilized foe were coupled with doubt and conceptual slippage. The authorities in this instance show alternately concern and contempt for the brigand, and his death is a breach of the rules of decency, a blot on the army's conscience, a sullying encounter with the grotesque and a failed propaganda ceremony. The brigand is the pivotal point of ambivalent representations of the relationship between society and crime, between the nation and its as yet un-Italianized badlands. The Italian officer class, and many of the policy makers who gave them orders, saw themselves both as taking a childlike population in hand in the cause of educating them in citizenship, and as fighting a subhuman enemy of the nation with the most self-consciously ruthless means.

Pasquale Villari and the genesis of the Southern question

The Southern question which a small group of intellectuals sought to pose to the ruling class of Italy in the decades after Unification was a national question. It was national not in the sense that it preoccupied broad sections of the population, or even of the governing élite, but because it was thought as a subset of another group of issues which concerned nation-building, how regional and national cultures were related and how Italy might progress and compete with other countries.

Pasquale Villari, a historian of Neapolitan origin who taught at universities in Tuscany, did more than anyone to set in place the ideological infrastructure of the Southern question in the years of the *Destra*. Villari had been attempting to bring the

problems of the South into public view since 1861. His
'Southern letters' of 1875 were acknowledged to have inspired
a generation of campaigners for the South.[26] But it is the
essays 'Di che è la colpa?' ('Who is to blame?') of 1866
(occasioned by the military defeats of Custoza and Lissa) and
'La scuola e la questione sociale in Italia' ('Schools and the
social question in Italy') of 1872 which can give the clearest
image of the coalescing of the many political and cultural
influences that characterized the first formulations of the
Southern question. Villari's work can tell us a great deal about
the patterns of assumption and disquiet which produced the
demand for the kind of dispassionate observation of the
poverty of the Southern poor for which the first *meridionalisti*
are best known. What follows is a reconstitution of the patriotic
conceptual framework that Villari set down for the social
question, with particular attention to the place of the South in
it. My interpretation of Villari is conceived as an implicit
polemic against empirically based readings which have tended
to see in Villari and those influenced by him examples of, as
Asor Rosa puts it, 'moral and scientific seriousness'.[27] It is not,
of course, that I wish to cast a blanket of scepticism over
Villari's findings. Rather I hope by questioning the ahistorical
transparency, implicitly imputed by such judgements to the
notions of the moral and the scientific, to permit more
nuanced readings of these important texts.

Massimo Salvadori has remarked on the fact that the
Southern question was first posed, not by a politician or an
economist, but by a moralist.[28] But Salvadori does not specify
what exactly it meant to be a moralist. For Villari's concerns
were not specifically ethical; rather his sphere of competence
was the national character. The enabling assumption of what
could be called the moralist genre is a direct translatability
between, and even a conflation of, the properties of the
individual and the collectivity: 'A civilized nation is one which
has schools which, while they educate, also fortify the
individual intelligence, multiply the national intelligence, form
the character, give moral and civil discipline and improve the
whole man.'[29] The homology is expressible in corporeal terms,
as is demonstrated by Villari's habitual resorting to medical

analogies for national problems and by his occasional use of racial vocabulary within a Lamarckian framework. Villari's 'national moral character' manifests itself in the conduct of waiters and shopkeepers, and interrelates with historical events on the grand scale. It is formed by the most minute practices of education and upbringing as it is in the national experience of war, yet without it the successful functioning of military and educational machinery is impossible. It is regulated from above by the state, and in turn it informs and controls the state in its manifestation as public opinion.

The moralist is an authoritative dispenser of ethnic stereo-types, and of exhortations to the nation in the first person plural. Villari's favourite such exhortation, and the one which informs the entire ideological project of the Southern question, is that Italy must find a new ideal, a new sense of its identity, through the social question. Italy must rediscover its true character by knowing itself. His own work can be seen as an effort to begin the task of building an Italian knowledge of Italy. Hence the first stage of putting new backbone into the enervated national body is 'that of taking upon ourselves the task of laying bare our own sores, of destroying national illusions or prejudices.'[30]

Villari's project for an Italian knowledge of Italy involves a particular view of language. Long passages in 'Di chi è la colpa?' are directed against the 'bureaucratic formalism' of Italian society. 'La scuola e la questione sociale' goes as far as to dismiss writing itself as a 'fictitious' obstruction preventing a character-forming confrontation with reality:

> If the hour of sacrifice does not begin, the hour of true liberty will never arrive. We can only have an ephemeral and fictitious shadow of liberty: laws, codes, regulations, everything that is written on paper, nothing of the forces of the spirit which alone can redeem us. . . . It is facts and not words that teach morals.[31]

Empirical observation, therefore, has a function in Villari which is less cognitive than moral, in the sense I have outlined. Villari's social question has as much to do with creating an imaginary solidarity of the nation as it does with concrete knowledge.

Naples is the place in which the quintessentially patriotic act of knowing Italy is carried out. In 'Di chi è la colpa?' Villari's call to penetrate into the heart of Naples emblematizes the measures necessary for the moral regeneration of Italy:

> Is it perhaps nature which has made us so inferior? Or is it not rather upbringing and education, received and transmitted from generation to generation? In other countries it is upbringing and education which have improved the faculties and habits of every social class and perfected the whole man.
>
> So don't think only about reading and writing. Enter the city of Naples, leave the streets where the cultivated and well-to-do people live, where the rich and splendid carriages run; penetrate, instead, into the most remote quarters, where the alleyways and the din are so confused and intertwined, and the houses so tall and close together, that they form a labyrinth where not even the air, let alone anything else, can circulate freely.[32]

Naples and the South are, for Villari as for the campaigners who followed his lead, the paradigmatic theatre of a nation-building empirical knowledge, the ultimate test of the moral fibre of the Liberal élite.

Colonial or Oriental images appear intermittently in Villari's texts on the South, suggesting a conflict between his attempts to define the South and its problems as a national concern, and a tendency to think of the South, and particularly the Southern peasantry, as being beyond Italy.[33] Furthermore, Villari argues that, to be 'Italianized', the South must be studied. Yet his understanding of what it means to study different cultures is heavily influenced by a positivist teleology of science and a conception of history as a progression through a sequence of levels of civilization.[34] Although Villari argues a case for the South, not being barbaric, the binary opposition civility–barbarism and a social and evolutionary model of history inform his whole understanding of the Southern question and its relation to the national culture. The words Villari puts into the mouth of the Southern poor show the *Mezzogiorno* to be locked into a death struggle with Italy, a fight between opposing ends of the evolutionary scale: 'Either you manage to make us civilized, or we will manage to make you barbaric.'[35]

Elsewhere in Villari, it would seem that, to be fully 'Italian', all the country has to do is to recognize the fleeting, authentic, unselfconscious *italianità* in the marginal cultures which are its favoured objects of knowledge: 'Italy . . . does not need to fight to get merit; it only needs to know itself, and to make known the treasure it always keeps hidden.'[36] There is what one could call a poetics to Villari's *meridionalismo* which needs to make of the South both an Other and the raw stuff of the nation, the promise of the country's rise to the uplands of civilization. Italy can know and moralize itself, even place itself beyond language in the concrete reality of the poverty that preoccupies it, by investigating the Otherness it has invested in the South. Throughout Villari's work Italy is to constitute its identity by finding in the South both its Other and its most intimate self; its greatest 'moral danger'[37] and its ultimate salvation.

The power of the picturesque

The *Illustrazione Italiana* provides excellent source-material on which to base a study of the more general representations of the South that were current in the broader culture between 1880 and 1900. The leading illustrated magazine of its day, it spearheaded a drive by Treves, one of the largest publishing houses in the country, to carve out a middle-level market across Italy for its products.[38]

In its presentation of the South the *Illustrazione Italiana* displays a striking obsession with the picturesque. In an article dating from July 1882, for example, Nicola Lazzaro narrates a visit to Capri and is disappointed by the rundown parts of town:

> However on the shore, the full poetry of the place returns as one sees groups of children who, half-covered in rags, very grimy, squatting on the ground or sitting on benches and stones, adopt various picturesque poses as they enjoy the breeze or the sunlight—they almost always live off a sweet idleness.[39]

The picturesque was repeatedly found, as here, in even the most obvious poverty: the *Illustrazione Italiana* had a remark-

1.   '. . . groups of children who . . . live off a sweet idleness.'
(*Illustrazione Italiana*, 16 July 1882, 44)

able capacity to aestheticize social problems (see plate 1). In focusing on the picturesque however, the magazine was not just drawing a consolatory veil over an ugly or alien reality: the picturesque and associated terms form a systematic field of connotation which it is my aim to explore here.

The *Illustrazione Italiana* was characterized by a celebratory brand of patriotism: it had a limitless appetite for images of the king and queen and for the many new patriotic monuments and rites of Umbertian Italy. But just as important as the reproduction of public symbols of *italianità* ('Italian-ness') was the fostering of a private patriotic awareness through the languages of art and literature. What primarily concerns me here is the magazine's normative images of middle-level culture, its efforts to construct a model sensibility. For if the *Illustrazione Italiana* was to sell to a national market, then it had to tap into and cultivate national sentiment; it had to make stereotypes of Italy as it competed for readers. My case is that representations of the South as picturesque had a central place in that project.

In 1885, as part of a subscription drive for a sister publication, *Margherita*, which was aimed at women, the *Illustrazione Italiana*, published an advertisement with the offer of a free print by Vincenzo Caprile (see plate 2). The text of the advertisement proclaims the offer in terms that constitute something of a lesson in taste:

A painting has now become the necessary ornament of our drawing-rooms, and taste, which is day by day becoming more exquisitely artistic, demands that a painting should have a true value; it is not enough for it to reproduce an elegant and pleasant subject, but, in the intonation of its colour, in the movement of its figures, it must also give one that pleasurable impression that arises only from the works of the true artists, those who portray truth, not only with skill, but also with talent.[40]

To have real value, to be part of the ever more artistic progress of taste, we are told, a picture must provide the unmistakable (yet inexpressible) *frisson* of true art. In other words, what the *Illutrazione Italiana*'s projected reader demands of art is that it

2.   'A painting has now become the necessary ornament of our
drawing-rooms . . .'.
(*Illustrazione Italiana*, 29 November 1885, 352)

be recognizably 'arty'. What the magazine peddles is a type of kitsch that can be tightly defined: it consists of texts and images whose meaning is predominantly a proclamation of their own status as traditional high culture. As well as being a marketing strategy, a taste for kitsch is the distinguishing mark that was used to identify the readers of the magazine as a discerning public. Yet as such, that taste also became one of the key registers through which Italy's uncultured elements were understood. Social change at the end of the nineteenth century had as its concomitant a constant self-definition on the part of Italy's upper social strata. The *Illustrazione Italiana*'s cult of the artistic should be interpreted as one aspect of the production of a patriotic middle-class cultural identity through the representation of that which lay beyond the boundaries of the nation—what the magazine called its 'elegant and cultivated public'—yet within the confines of the nation–state. It is significant that the subject of the print in the subscription offer is an idealized Southern peasant woman: 'How pleasant that *pacchiana* is; she is cheerful, healthy, clean, with her flesh blooming with splendid health, with a smile pure and sincere, with a joke ready at her lips!'[41] The picturesque is the name for the *Illustrazione Italiana*'s cherished artistic qualities when they are projected onto the poor, and predominantly the Southern poor. The function of the picturesque is to refresh and reflect back the artistic common values of the magazine and its readers, but it also has functions related to patriotism.

In 1882 the six-hundredth anniversary of the Sicilian Vespers was celebrated. The *Illustrazione*'s coverage typifies a number of features of its outlook, such as its conversion of regional histories into a calendar of patriotic ceremonies. Raffaello Barbiera's account of the festivities contains all of the themes that characterize the magazine's aestheticizing brand of nationalism. The article contains many references to the artistic charms of the buildings and countryside of the locality, but the most significant appeal to the common points of reference provided by high art is in relation to the masses:

An unbelievable feeling of poetry animates this people. The verses of Tasso's *Gerusalemme liberata*, amongst other things, are

continually illustrated on the carts which haul heaps of enormous cabbages or stones from the mountains which crown
Palermo. And the beautiful Clorinda, and Goffredo and
Tancredi, and other knights are living, painted with rough
brushes on the panels of those vehicles which perform the
function of illustrated novels: mobile novels, the delight of the
wretched people who still do not know how to read.[42]

The *Illustrazione Italiana*'s preferred positive stereotype of the
lower orders endows them with a crude aesthetic quality of
which they themselves are unaware: in this case, they display
precocious signs of artistic awareness whose full meaning can
only be grasped by those who have read Tasso; by those, like
the magazine's readers, who have a fully developed artistic and
patriotic culture. Garibaldi's popularity in Palermo is shown,
in the same article, to be a precie analogue of such
spontaneous creativity in the political field. He appeals to the
riotous imagination of the people, inspiring a loyalty empty of
political content. Of the moment when the parade arrives at
the church where the medieval rebellion broke out, Barbiera
writes:

> And how 'Michelangelesque' [*michelangiolesco*] was that multi-
> tude of common people who, panting, had, against every
> prohibition, got past the gates and invaded the avenues of the
> cemetery in a confused mass; Michelangelesque when, in a
> flash, the multitude stopped to hear what one citizen was
> shouting his lungs out at them from atop a stairway; and it was
> still more so when, begged by him to clear the area in the name
> of Garibaldi, that mob shook its arms, threw its berets in the air
> and started to bellow 'Long live Garibaldi!' as it retreated.[43]

The word that most often encapsulates this elementary,
aesthetic *italianità* is 'picturesque'. A picturesque scene,
custom or figure is foreign enough to be exotic, to belong to
the poetic margin beyond a humdrum reality, and yet familiar
enough to be soothingly Italian. To be picturesque is to be
childlike, to have a gauche fondness for the simple pleasures of
colour and noise; it is to surprise and delight the onlooker with
how unknowingly mature one can be; it is to be constantly
amazed and constantly trusting; it is to suffer and not

understand why; it is to be ruled by the benign power of spectacle.

In the *Illustrazione Italiana* the South and its people exist primarily as a display case of fragments of superseded cultures and as the privileged arena for the bucolic experience: it is the site of innumerable moments of contemplative reverie. The magazine's fixation with the picturesque persists even during episodes such as the revolt of the Sicilian Fasci: 'But the poet, the painter and the artist will always admire those people, who now quiver in their suffering, as they boil over an stir themselves up. The picturesque, the poetic never deserts them.'[44]

The function of the picturesque is governed by its relation to sets of antithetically constructed categories that structure the middle-class view of the world in the *Illustrazione Italiana*. The picturesque names, aestheticizes and patronizingly celebrates the South's aomalous position between Italy and the Orient, between the world of civilized progress and the spheres of either rusticity or barbarism. One of its tasks is to move the South nearer to 'us' when it is pastoral and nearer to 'them' when it is uncivilized. For example, in a later article on the disturbances in Sicily, the reporter tells how he photographed a town crier announcing the proclamation of the government's 'state of siege' to the people (see plate 3):

> You'll see! A real muezzin calling the faithful to prayer from the top of his mosque! Yes, because here the Saracen stamp is at its clearest and most obvious. In the fields where I interviewed many peasants I found only types with the most unmistakable African origin. My, how much strange intelligence there is in those muddled brains![45]

Orientalist imagery is frequently used to describe the South, although the Orient to which the South is compared is most often a land of mystery and imagination rather than of alien savagery. Yet writers on the Fasci seem to need at moments to resort to a language of extremity, typically borrowed from the colonial or Oriental context, with which to rule off a margin of irreducible, incomprehensible Otherness proper to the activities of the islanders. In the pages of the *Illustrazione Italiana* there is precious little middle ground for the South

3.   '. . . the South's anomalous position between Italy and the Orient . . .'.
(*Illustrazione Italiana*, 28 January 1894, 51)

between the quaint and the weird, the picturesquely Italian and the grotesquely Oriental.

Francesco Crispi's *sicilianità*

Francesco Crispi was the first Southerner to hold the office of prime minister. He dominated the Italian political scene for a turbulent decade after 1887, years of profound economic and political crisis that saw the 'social question' become open social conflict. For some time there has been a historical debate on the question of Crispi's public persona. The importance of this issue is that it concerns the timing and nature of the transition from oligarchic politics to mass politics in Italy. Denis Mack Smith and Silvio Lanaro, for example, have seen Crispi as a charismatic figure and have interpreted that charisma as an irrational or subconscious influence exercised over a mass audience.[46] But the precise means of communication of that influence, and the precise extent of his sway over the 'masses', have yet to be investigated. The admittedly rather easier task of studying the content of Crispi's patriotic ideology, in particular his mythologization of the *Risorgimento*, has been dealt with at greater length.[47] However, one important aspect of Crispi's public persona, his *sicilianità* or *meridionalità* (his 'Sicilian-ness' or 'Southern-ness') (this imprecision derives from the historical sources), has tended to be neglected. One group over whom Crispi undoubtedly did exercise considerable imaginative influence was the middle classes. What I intend to argue here is that, in so far as Crispi's charisma was felt by the middle classes, and particularly by their minor (and some not so minor) intellectuals, it cannot fully be understood without understanding the meanings of his *sicilianità*, seen as a cultural construct rather than as a biographical given. As the Sicilian constitutionalist Giorgio Arcoleo wrote in a portrait of Crispi published in 1905, Sicily was a plaçe 'where the race, like the soil, offers contrasts: it is both northern and Oriental; here it is Greece, there it is Africa; here it is a Nation, there it is a tribe'.[48]

The cultural context in which Crispi's image was formed needs to be carefully reconstructed. One important com-

ponent of that context is the language of antiparliamentarism
and political crisis. The spectacle of inefficiency, jobbery and
corruption in the workings of the Liberal parliament sickened
many Italians. The political programmes that incorporated a
critique of the parliamentary system were many and varied.
But it is striking that frustration with governmental
mechanisms frequently found its most loaded metaphors in
images of Otherness. The putative centre of Italy's political life
was often portrayed as being taken over by forces—such as
women, crowds and the *camorra*—associated with its un-
savoury margins. Scipio Sighele, a pioneer of 'crowd theory',
maintained that parliamentarism was best understood in the
terms of crowd psychology, as a pathological form of group
delinquency. He also argued that 'the Chamber . . . is psycho-
logically a woman and often a hysterical woman at that'.[49] The
imaginary South could provide plenty of grotesque stereotypes
of political behaviour: ostentatious feudal power; unchained
violence; a people who were congenitally incapable of obeying
the ground rules of the Liberal polity. Images of a Southern
Otherness were applied to parliament in, for example, Achille
Bizzoni's antiparliamentary novel *L'onorevole* of 1895: the
chamber is described as a 'malaria hospital' and the seat of
government as 'the great lazaret of the plague-ridden politicians who are now infecting the whole of Italy'.[50]

But the meanings of the imaginary South were highly
ambivalent. The verso of the South of brigandage, corruption
and malaria was a land of elemental but undisciplined
nationalistic dynamism, which could be seen, by figures such
as Turiello and d'Annunzio, as offering a positive contrast to
the ankylotic institutions.[51] Southern Italy could be valorized
in very similar terms to those often used to explain its problems—in Turiello's case, the supposedly artistic, undisciplined,
over-emotional temperament of its people. Going even further,
writers such as Sighele argued that liberal policies had in fact
been based on a mistaken application of northern European
principles when Italy as a whole was actually Latin or southern
nation which lived according to the dictates of irrational
forces, swinging between anarchy and servility. What I am
trying to show with these brief examples is that the peak of

Crispi's power coincided with a time when the threatened arrival of new social forces on the political stage created a crisis not only in society, but in conceptions of the nation. In the 1880s and 1890s it became increasingly difficult, and yet increasingly urgent, to conflate, in the name of the nation or the people, the interests of the country as a whole with those of the thin social stratum entrusted with the franchise. In that climate, notions of the national character, myths of the masses, ethnic stereotypes and a feeling of political crisis tended to converge on the figure of Crispi.

Some idea of Crispi's public persona among the middle and upper classes can be reconstructed through the many pamphlets, poems, biographies and monographs dealing with his life and politics. One typical text is by Guido Pieragnoli, published in 1887, in which even associations with Africa and a fevered imagination are positive effects of Crispi's Sicilian background:

> his native climate and the blazing noontides of the African sea contributed to waking ever more powerfully in his blood and in his imagination that ardour and those fevers which were then to drive him in his adventurous life, and they tempered into inflexible resolution that character which was bound to, and did, make of Crispi one of the most eminent statesmen of his time.[52]

In the eyes of the middle classes the concept of a 'Sicilian statesman' was virtually a contradiction in terms. Writers on Crispi almost invariably identify the same paradox: he embodies qualities considered unorthodox or unofficial, indeed he is on the brink of being something other than Italian, and yet, as the most patriotic man in Parliament, he occupies a place in Italy's imaginary centre. Sicily and Crispi occupy a border zone where the imagined modern nation fades into an Africa or an Orient. Yet it is also where the nation hopes to find its origins, the most powerful, primeval qualities of *italianità*. Crispi, in short, is imagined as a frontiersman.

For the patrician Alessandro Guiccioli, Crispi 'embodied the most elevated principles' and yet ethnic stereotypes created a mystique around him: 'he does not carry out his business in the town square, but in the reserved and mysterious way characteristic of old conspirators and Sicilians.'[53] One journalist attributes the extraordinary appeal of Crispi to his faith in himself, a faith that reaches the point of superstition as is illustrated by the amulets he always carried: 'he is not a Southerner for nothing.'[54] Crispi's perceived strength is admixed with strangeness. But it is striking that almost all of the positive characteristics attributed to Crispi are versions of more derogatory ethnic stereotypes: eulogy from Sicily and execration from Milan are composed from different connotations of the same language, although Crispi's supporters can refer far more freely to 'his known characteristic of being a true Sicilian in the full sense of the word'.[55]

The 'people' over whom Crispi is imagined to exert such a strange influence is a very flexible notion: it is a concept that can be used to erase divisions between the masses and the upper strata, yet in doing so it betrays the ideological anxieties of those strata. For Giorgio Siculo, the country needs a strong leader like Crispi because 'we have not got much in the way of a political upbringing; in too many respects it is either unformed or has to be reformed. We pass very easily from one extreme to the other.'[56] Crispi is widely perceived to have a mysterious power over, and affinity with, an alternately unruly and servile nation.

In 1895 Leone Fortis, a journalist whose magazine columns became something of an institution, wrote a monograph on Crispi. For Fortis, Crispi's relations with public opinion are characterized by 'ups and downs which resemble the alternating outbreaks of anger and peace between two lovers'. He was particularly acclaimed during the outbreak of '*our* excessive and neurotic Italian impressionability' following the defeat at Dogali.[57] Crispi's attraction for the people is bodily, jealous, irrational: his charisma prevails upon a feminized nation.

There is something of the same ambivalence in the constant comparisons of Crispi to a volcano: he is both picturesque and powerful; a symbol of Italy and a metonym of the un-Italian South; an uncontrollable force of nature and a vital energy at the heart of the national culture. Crispi, the saviour of the institutions, has an implied affinity with vital and dangerous forces in the nation outside those institutions. As we have seen, those dangerous forces can be constructed by association with the masses, and even with the feminine, but most consistently with the imaginary South.

The two cartoons of Crispi reproduced on plates 4 and 5 provide a useful encapsulation of some of the images with which Crispi was associated. Plate 4 is by Teja and deals with Crispi's famous Turin speech in October 1887. Augusto Ferrero comments on the cartoon as follows:

> [Crispi] today finds the same flexibility in the necks of Parliament and the country as Depretis once did. Everyone gathers faithfully around him, everyone bows before him . . . Faith is a fine thing, says Teja: but it must not become fanaticism which leads, as with the Muslims, to self-abnegation in the form of servility and suicide.[58]

For all Crispi's patriotism, his influence is perceived as being distinctly alien; it is the volatile, irrational sway of an Oriental despot or a cult leader; it brings out a highly dangerous submissiveness in both Parliament and people. The Arab world is a familiar source of ethnocentric images of pomp and fanaticism, but it also has associations, as we have seen in the *Illustrazione Italiana*, with the South and particularly with Sicily.

Plate 5, which depicts Crispi showing a Moroccan delegation around his own personal museum, is from *Il Fischietto* in January of 1890. The items in the background of the cartoon are Garibaldi's red coat (a reminder of Crispi's past as a republican man of action); the Three Graces (an allusion to his three wives and to the charges of bigamy that had been levelled against him); elephants' tusks (symbolizing his ambitions for Italian expansion in Africa); and Bismarck's coat (Crispi's admiration for and imitation of the German statesman was well known). Crispi is seen concluding the visit by proudly showing the Moroccans his giant horn amulet of coral, a symbol of Southern superstition:

> 'Here, gentlemen, is the secret of *my* great power, *my* talisman against *my* enemies . . . I show it sometimes but it never leaves

4.   'La fede è una bella cosa, purchè non giunga a tanta abnegazione'
['Faith is a fine thing . . . but it must not become fanaticism . . .'].
(*Teja* published originally in *Il Pasquino*, 23 October 1887)

5.   La visite des Marocains à Crispi [The Moroccans visit Crispi].
(published originally in *Il Fischietto*, 21 January 1890)

me.' And at this, the flabbergasted ambassadors cried out to one other: 'Sir, may Allah keep it safe for you for a long time yet!'[59]

Here it is as if Crispi is comparing notes on superstitious authority with visitors from a culture that was a byword for pseudo-religion and tyranny: Crispi moves in the same world as the Arab, a world where the domains of government and irrational faith are confused.

For the middle classes Crispi was an uncanny figure: he was both beyond the pale marked out by motifs normally associated with the nation and, as a statesman and great patriot, he occupied a privileged place inside it. He was perceived to be both of the other Italy and a rampart against it, as he was a politician considered to be above or against politics. These two-sided understandings have their counterpart in conceptions of the masses as, alternately, loyal or even zealous *popolo* ('people') and disorderly mob; as potential Northern European citizens or as incurable Latin minions. Equally ambivalent are the images used to describe the Parliament over which Crispi rules: it is at once the centre of the nation and a corrupting force from its underside. Political debate within the political class in the years of economic, social and political crisis after 1887 was fraught with fears. Faced by what the *Illustrazione Italiana* called 'strange, incredible conflicts'[60] on the nation's frontiers, and by lurid crime, violent popular disorder and Byzantine corruption at its centre, I would maintain that the middle classes found in Crispi's *sicilianità* a way of thinking the situation as well as a means of creating concrete political strategies to deal with it.

Conclusions

The kind of representations examined here are not, as regionalism, opposed to the nation-building aspirations and patriotic sentiments of the élites of post-Unification Italy. They are, rather, functions of those aspirations and sentiments. At a fundamental level my readings have been premised on an awareness of the ideological function of nationalist discourse as a set of ways of at once thinking and disavowing social divisions. The *Mezzogiorno* constituted both a problem and a resource for the patriotic imagery of the post-Unification bourgeoisie. the cases of Villari, the *Illustrazione Italiana* and Crispi show how the South provided the opportunity for the question of the relations between élites and masses to be transposed onto a geographical axis, to be worked at and worried about in the terms of ethnicity and geography. The South was, to use a literary term, an imaginatively charged synecdoche of the problem of nation-building.

I hope that these four very different aspects of a vast amount of material have give some impression of what I believe was not a rigid or static mindset of the bourgeoisie towards the South. In none of these contexts, even in a magazine as crass as the *Illustrazione Italiana*, is the construction of the South as Other the drawing of a once-and-for all Manichaean distinction between Italy and the South. This is so not least because representations of the South rely on a semantic mobility in terms such as 'brigandage', 'the picturesque', and indeed 'the South' itself. There was, moreover, a traffic in representations of the *Mezzogiorno* between the levels and spheres of the culture of the upper and middle classes, between those places and times when the questions of the nation and the South were posed together.

Some reflections on the relation my kind of approach bears to the fundamental debate about nation-building in Italy are perhaps an appropriate way to end. These analyses of ethnocentrism towards the South make only a minimal contribution to the history of state-formation: the subject at hand has been how those who used the language of nationalism viewed the country beyond, and not the concrete means by which the use of that language was made more widespread. Yet nation-building is more than a concrete process of institutional change. A history of nation-building, as well as describing the social transformations that encourage the spread of national sentiment, must address the crucial question of how patriotism is then lived out, of how the available nationalist jargons are appropriated and activated. Moreover, any given project to Italianize sections of the population, such as was involved in legitimating the war against brigandage or incorporated into the presentation of the *Illustrazione Italiana*, cannot happen without the slippery terminologies of nationalism, terminologies which are always used to differentiate as well as to integrate. My studies might be seen to constitute examples of how the nation is constantly 'rebuilt' in discourse. The discursive aspects of nation-building are just as dense and problematic whether one's object of study is would-be nation-builders, as it is here, or their target audience; they can only be tackled by studies prepared to engage with the close and shifting texture of national identity.

NOTES

1. A. Niceforo, *L'Italia barbara contemporanea (Studi ed appunti)* (Milan–Palermo, 1898), 3.
2. A. Gramsci, *Il Risorgimento* (Rome, 1975), 99.
3. M. Salvadori, *Il mito del buongoverno. La questione meridionale da Cavour a Gramsci* (Turin, 1963), 189.
4. Niceforo, *L'Italia barbara*, 4.
5. E. Said, *Orientalism* (Harmondsworth, 1978), 322.
6. Niceforo, *L'Italia barbara*, 17.
7. See, for example, F. Fonzi, *Crispi e lo 'stato di Milano'*, (Milan, 1965), and D. Mack Smith, 'Regionalism', *Modern Italy. A Topical History since 1861* eds, E. Tannenbaum and E. Noether (New York, 1974).
8. Niceforo, *L'Italia barbara*, 292.
9. Ibid., 6.
10. A. Giddens, *The Nation-State and Violence* (Cambridge, 1985), vol. 2 of *A Contemporary Critique of Historical Materialism*, 219.
11. B. Anderson, *Imagined Communities. Reflections on the Origin and Spread of Nationalism* (London, 1983).
12. Niceforo, *L'Italia barbara*, 296.
13. R. Romanelli, *L'Italia Liberale (1860–1900)* (Bologna, 1979), 10.
14. This essay represents a sample of a much longer piece of work: 'Representations of the Mezzogiorno in Post-Unification Italy (1860–1900)', doctoral thesis, University of Sussex, 1993.
15. See J. Dickie, 'A Word at War: the Italian Army and *Brigandage*, 1860–70', *History Workshop* 33 (1992) 1–24. The article was also published in Italy (not without mistranslations) in *Passato e Presente*, 26 (1991), 53–74. See also the subsequent debate on brigandage between L. Riall and J. Dickie in the next two issues of *Passato e Presente*, 27 (1991), 195–8, and 28 (1993), 193–95.
16. A. Bianco di Saint Jorioz, *Il brigantaggio alla frontiera pontificia, 1860–3* (Milan, 1864), 9.
17. A. Saffi, *Inchiesta sul brigantaggio*, ed. T. Pedio (Manduria, 1983), 61.
18. Letter dated 23 November 1863 from the advocate-general in Turin to

146   JOHN DICKIE

the military tribunal in Chieti, *Archivio Centrale dello Stato, Tribunali Militari. Brigantaggio. Provincie meridionali,* 127/1424.

19. N. Bixio, *Epistolario,* 2 (Rome, 1942), 143.
20. L.C. Farini, *Carteggi: la liberazione del Mezzogiorno e la formazione del Regno d'Italia,* 3 (Bologna, 1952), 208.
21. Letter dated 28 May 1865, *Archivio Centrale,* 193 (miscellaneous correspondence).
22. Ibid.
23. Ibid.
24. Ricasoli to La Marmora (24 October 1861) and La Marmora to Ricasoli (2 February 1862), both in A. La Marmora, *Carteggi,* (Turin, 1928), 115, 141.
25. Letter dated 18 June 1865, *Archivio Centrale.*
26. See P. Villari, *Le lettere meridionali e altri scritti sulla questione sociale,* 2nd edn (Turin, 1885).
27. A. Asor Rosa, *La cultura,* in *Storia d'Italia,* vol. 4, *Dall'Unità a oggi,* 2 (Turin, 1975), 920.
28. M. Salvadori, *Il mito del buongoverno,* 34.
29. P. Villari, 'Di chi è la colpa', *Lettere meriodionali,* 296–7.
30. Ibid, 290.
31. P. Villari, 'La scuola e la questione sociale', *Lettere meridionali,* 203–4.
32. P. Villari, 'Di chi è la colpa?' *Lettere meridionali,* 300.
33. In P. Villari, *Lettere meridionali'* for example, there is the following account:

[The peasant] might kneel before his master with the same feeling with which the Indian adores the storm or the lightning. But if ever the day came when this spell was broken, the peasant would rise up to avenge himself with his long-repressed hatred, with his brutal passions. Sometimes, indeed, those hordes of slaves have been seen to transform themselves instantly into hordes of cannibals.

(p. 57)

Naturally the precise relation between images of this kind and the more soberly analytical moments of Villari's texts needs to be reconstructed with care.

34. See M. Cicalese, *Note per un profilo di Pasquale Villari,* Istituto storico italiano per l'età moderna e contemporanea (1979), 58, on the relation between Villari's patriotic discourse and his conception of history.
35. P. Villari, *Lettere meridionali,* 70.
36. P. Villari, *Le prime lettere meridionali,* (Rome, 1920), 62.
37. P. Villari, 'La scuola e la questione sociale in Italia', *Lettere meridionali,* 173.
38. Research into the *Illustrazione Italiana* is hampered by the absence of circulation figures and other commercial documentation relating to it.
39. *Illustrazione Italiana,* 16 July 1882, 44.
40. *Illustrazione Italiana,* 29 November 1885, 352.
41. A *pacchiana* is a Southern peasant woman in traditional costume.
42. *Illustrazione Italiana,* 16 April 1881, 275.
43. Ibid.
44. *Illustrazione Italiana,* 12 November 1893, 311.

45. *Illustrazione Italiana*, 28 January 1894, 51.
46. D. Mack Smith, *Italy—A Modern History*, (Michigan, 1959), 140, and S. Lanaro, *L'Italia nuova* (Turin, 1988), 151–2. Lanaro's reading is suggestive, but over-reliant on a Weberian model of charisma, which ceases to be analytically useful the moment it invokes the 'irrational' nature of charismatic influence. The point about such influence, as with other emotions, is surely that it has its own form of logic.
47. See U. Levra, 'Il Risorgimento nazional-popolare di Crispi', *Fare gli Italiani. Memoria e celebrazione del Risorgimento*, Comitato di Torino dell'Istituto per la Storia del Risorgimento Italiano (1992), 299–386.
48. G. Arcoleo, *Francesco Crispi* (Milan, 1905), 9.
49. S. Sighele, 'contro il parlamentarismo', *La delinquenza settaria* (Milan, 1897), 259.
50. A. Bizzoni, *L'onorevole* (Milan, 1895), 272, 229.
51. See G. d'Annunzio, *Le vergini delle rocce* (Milan, 1978), and also the figure of Cesare Bronte (Crispi) in d'annunzio's *Gloria* (1899) in *Tutte le opere, Tragedie sogni e misteri* 1 (Milan, 1968). See also P. Turiello, *Governo e governati in Italia* (Turin, 1980), and *Il secolo XIX* (Bologna, 1947).
52. G. Pieragnoli, *Francesco Crispi* (Rome, 1887), 8.
53. Quoted in D. Farini, *Diario di fine secolo* (Rome, 1961), entry for 9 December 1893, 176–7.
54. L. Fortis, *Francesco Crispi* (Rome, 1895), 11.
55. B. Galletti, *L'attualità e l'onorevole Francesco Crispi* (Palermo, 1890), 42–3.
56. G. Siculo, *Francesco Crispi a Torino* (Turin, 1887), 35.
57. L. Fortis, *Francesco Crispi*, S, 8 (emphasis added).
58. 'Il ritorno del tappeto dalla Mecca, dipinto da Teja', originally published in *Il Pasquino*, 23 October 1887, reproduced here from A. Ferrero, ed., *Caricature di Teja (dal Pasquino)* (Turin, 1900), 284.
59. Originally published in *Il Fischietto*, 21 January 1890, and reproduced here from J. Grand-Carteret, *Crispi, Bismarck et la Triple Alliance en caricatures* (Paris, 1891), 217. My translation of the accompanying text is from Grand-Carteret's French translation of the original, which I have not as yet located.
60. *Illustrazione Italiana*, 14 January 1894, 18. The reference is to the Sicilian Fasci.

7

The Nationalization of Politics and the Politicization of the Nation in Liberal Italy

FULVIO CAMMARANO

The title of this chapter is not a simple play on words, as I would like to stress how the concept of the nation itself is actually subject to full acceptance of the undisputed primacy of what is 'political'. The category of 'political' redefines the relationships among individuals, within a specific geographical area, as exclusively formal political bonds, usually governs by a constitution. Historically we could say that the process of politicization of a nation is the attempt to realize this ideal. It means, in other words, transforming the real bonds and social conflicts among the nation's actors into purely political relationships, to which all other affinities are subordinate. We must therefore evaluate the phenomenon of the nationalization of politics—that is the construction of a single political framework throughout Italy—against the process of politicization—the diffusion and enforcement of this political system. This system should be considered (as Farneti proposed) as a system that attempts to disentangle itself from the web of relationships of civil society, by creating an autonomous power network, (naturally a legitimate and efficient one), which is able to reconcile the internal conflicts of society in specifically political terms.[1]

Moving from this ideal to the reality of Italian history in the Liberal period, it is evident that this process did not occur through a constant elimination of the expressions of actual power, nor was it a chance development in the gap between modernising sectors that sought to formalize the new rules and traditional sectors determined to preserve actual power structures, with all that entailed.

Many recent studies have acknowledged the weakness of an explanatory approach based on the hypothesis of a one-sided hierarchical relationship between an 'equalizing' centre, by definition 'political' and modern, and an unyielding periphery, characterized by parochiality and backwardness. That is why an inquiry into the roles, merits and limitations of the Liberal ruling class in their attempt to nurture a national view of politics, must focus on the relationship between the consolidation of national institutions and the process of emancipation of the political system as a whole.

This problem has often been ignored by Italian historians as if the politicization of the nation were automatically a by-product of the formation of the state and the creation of a national market. In fact, as Raffaele Romanelli emphasized, the Liberal project appeared quite contradictory as early as the immediate aftermath of the Italian *Risorgimento*.[2] The ruling class was well aware that their task of giving the nation a collective identity had to include a rapid mass politicization of the population, especially the South. This was meant to be a project of a sort of 'education to freedom' and it was quite obvious that it would also involve a very dangerous revival of anti-system forces and encourage the legitimate demands of the clergy and the Democratic groups.

This, as Paolo Pombeni has recently written, was the reason why Liberals refused to view the party as an instrument for political intervention.[3] It is also why large sections of the national bourgeoisie chose the indirect and 'situational' power represented by the occupation of the state and public administration. This was a process of 'alienation from politics' that would greatly affect political life in Italy. Moderates and progressives encountered the same difficulties in trying to adopt a national political structure.[4] Their difficulties did not arise, as we previously thought, from cultural limitations: on the contrary these ruling classes had clearly understood the important role that a party could play. They believed, however, that politicizing the nation would lead to an irresistible social change and to the legitimation of emerging subcultures. Badaloni, a Socialist member of the Chamber of Deputies, was aware of this contradictory situation. In his parliamentary question about the Sicilian uprisings of 1894, he said:

> We see in the concept of national unity, of Italian unity, the progression of an historical process dictated by economic needs which replaced the medieval *comuni* with regional states and the latter with national entities, thus promoting the brotherhood of nations among mankind and uniting the concept of mankind with the concept of the motherland . . . You cannot charge us, Signor Crispi, with undermining the unity of our motherland. *You cannot accuse us of this.* Our party aims at setting up its structures within the boundaries of public liberty, we plan to become a majority, and you cannot deny us this right that we share with all other parties, unless you destroy all your laws.[5]

This speech points to the causes of the ending of the Liberals' delusion that, together with credit for Unification, they could claim for themselves the historical merit of having re-established a harmony between civil society and political society in the nineteenth century. They had believed that even if not all the historic problems had been resolved, at least a neutralization of the political context had taken place. The politicization of the country was therefore for late nineteenth-century Liberals the dark side of nationalization.

Immediately after Unification Parliament had been seen as the only legitimate political expression of the nation. To quote Cavour: 'I believe that the only representation of the people resides in this Chamber of Parliament . . . I believe it would be a great mistake today if the nation's true opinion is not faithfully represented here.'[6] Yet, especially after the impact of the extension of voting rights and the introduction of list voting in 1882, Parliament appeared to Liberals to be a particularistic body and a source of disintegration. Sonnino, too, believed that Parliament would be deprived of its dignity if its usefulness resided only in fulfilling the chronic need for reconciling conflicting local and individual interests, or if it was believed that the 'public administration' could only operate in a conflictual and combative environment.[7] During this period a whole generation of politicians, intellectuals and jurists began wondering about the best way to neutralize the process of politicization of the nation without slowing down the process of mass-nationalization.

From this perspective a symbolic event was the failure of Crispi's project, the last attempt to revive a self-confident Liberalism in the Jacobin–*Risorgimento* tradition. Crispi often made reference to the modernizing and anti-feudal features of the *Risorgimento*, and this enabled him to supply a disorientated Liberal bourgeoisie with some sort of identity based on a leading role for this social class in the completion of the process of modernization that had not been finished immediately after Unification due to the overwhelming obstacles it had encountered.[8] In 1891 Crispi wrote:

> The lower classes must remember that everything that has happened in Italy during this century was the work of the bourgeoisie; national unification, the independence of our motherland from the foreigner, the freedom of citizens, are all due to it. The lower classes must therefore be grateful to the bourgeoisie and must be content that they were given a place at life's banquet. The duties of the bourgeoisie have not yet been discharged, of course, and it is the duty of the bourgeoisie to pursue the social reorganization that will ensure for the working class the well-being that is due.[9]

Crispi aimed at achieving a 'positive' political identity, able to compete with those of the Catholics and Socialists. His commitment was not rewarded, however, because of the complexities of ongoing economic and social change, and because the bourgeoisie was historically denied the established channels of 'religion' and 'motherland' (the latter of which was also claimed by the spiritual heirs of Mazzini). During the late 1880s and early 1890s the gap between the national bourgeoisie and the ruling class became apparent. The only project of the ruling class for a political unification of the bourgeoisie was transformism, yet it had proved weak as a source of cultural legitimation and was unable to produce a bureaucratic set of rules that could provide a reliable frame of reference for the relationships among the social classes.[10] The overall failure of transformism did not result in any feasible alternative to political and parliamentary opportunism, nor an alternative to that bureaucratic discretionary power that was still a component of Giolitti's control of the nation's political mobilization. From the end of the century several members of the Italian Liberal intelligentsia began to seek a reshaping of politics. This was articulated as the need for a strengthening of the state as a reaction to the failure of the operation of elective institutions (Mosca, Turiello) or, by contrast, a confidence that a more coherent Liberalism would achieve the intent of integrating the popular masses (Pantaleoni, de Viti de Marco).

Both these projects required a renewed initiative and the construction of a high-profile ethical model. This way it would be possible to deal with the continuous, creeping process of politicization of the nation brought about day by day by Socialists and Catholics in municipal environments. In 1889 there had been a reform of local administration. Some political subcultures contained a strong ideological identification, and this enabled them to transform the *comuni* into headquarters for political projects, whereas previously they had been seen as dominated by notables, clienteles and restricted interest groups. It was a self-sustaining process that transformed local administrations into an inescapable component of national politics, and created a circuit closely binding together party organization, the local élite and the national Parliament.

The reforms of 1889 therefore definitively established that the administrative issue was a political question.[11] A new and dangerous area of conflict was opening up for the Liberal bourgeoisie in which any initiative resulted in the reflection of an ideological concept or a presumed political division. The fact that such a division was likely to be the result of a conflict between local interest groups, dating back to centuries before, was irrelevant. Behind the expressions of fatigue with politics and the eulogy of sound administration, typical of these years, there was no relaunch of particularism, but rather the desire to be a part of modernity, exploiting a strong municipal identification that would lead to better power relations with the centre.

The municipal arena thus took on the role of workshop where a new and wider political class was forged, the real core of political mediation that nationalist thinkers, not by accident, came to identify with the substance of Giolitti's approach.[12] The growth of the municipal dimension during Giolitti's rule embodied the institutionalization of social conflict and the acceptance of a principle for the redistribution of resources in favour of better organized forces. And this was exactly what detonated the nationalist reaction. Nationalism clearly perceived that the politicization of the nation would no longer come about through a conversion of the majority to 'public' reason or through a gradual automatic acceptance of the superiority of 'Liberal' institutions, along the lines of the old Jacobin model.

Nationalism turned the question around, and its response was substantially tautological: the masses were the nation, and the nation was the masses. The definition included the very bourgeoisie that Liberals saw as composed of individuals. Now the political system was not legitimized by its defence of individual right, but by social right. The twentieth-century aimed to be represented as part of the community. This was because Socialists, and to some degree Catholics, had shown that by being part of a strong community one could become a citizen. Community identification had nothing to do with the principles of Liberalism or the state of law. The nationalists' post-Liberalism had to find a common identity that could, at least by demagogic standards, to be defined as 'different'.[13] The old idea of 'nation' was therefore resurrected, but it was no longer a historical premise, rather the identity of individuals formed through war who were by now part of the masses. Thus the epitome of classical democracy, the ancient Greek *agora* ('market place') conquered by the Socialists who had brought back to it the art of politics, was now to be recovered as a symbolic place for the middle classes, and, at the same time, retained as the symbolic site of political supremacy. In 1914 Alfredo Rocco, the Nationalist leader who began his political life as a radical, recalled the power of this symbolic dimension:

'If the *piazza* [the town square] is an instrument for governing, it is a state apparatus: it is necessary for nationalists to use it in

order to pursue the vital interests of the nation, instead of
leaving it—as the other constitutional parties do—in the hands
of the enemies of the state and the nation.

In this way, while the subversives use crowds and uprisings
to overpower the state, we use the crowds and uprisings to
support the state.'[14]

Shortly afterwards, however, historical circumstances gave life
to an unexpected national *agora* that put an end to all
dichotomies between national and local patterns. Italy took
part in a war that the Nationalists had desired as a means to
create a compact hierarchical society. This would clearly
demonstrate that foreign policy counted far more than
domestic policy in finding a solution to the problem of limited
bourgeois hegemony. War was a new experience, in which the
nation would be, by and large, involved as a productive unit.
This allowed the use of that *piazza* or *agora* of the *polis* ('city'),
the mythical place for equalization and the legitimization of
identity, that had been sought without success in previous
years. The nation had now become a concrete experience for
all citizens. Yet, once again, there had been no nationalization
of politics, since the war also demonstrated how limited the
opportunities for access to decision-making were.

After the war the political unity of the nation became a truly
shared heritage. Male universal suffrage, freedom of political
organization and proportional representation were established.
Italian Liberalism was entitled to claim that it had solved the
historical problem of the nationalization of politics. This,
however, was done without taking into account the problem of
the politicization of the nation. Liberal Italy was shaping a
common language and a political tradition that was also
conflictual. The ruling class did not acknowledge this process
as a basic component of the political system, however, and
therefore did not accept the need to institutionalize it as a
legitimate political resource, which could be used to reconcile
the divisions in civil society.

NOTES

1. P. Farneti, *Sistema politico e società civile* (Turin, 1971); F. Cammarano,
'Nazionalizzazione della politica e politicizzazione della nazione. I

dilemmi della classe dirigente nell'Italia liberale', *Dalla città alla nazione. Borghesie ottocentesche in Italia e Germania*, eds, M. Merrigi and P. Schiera (Bologna, 1993), 139–63.

2. R. Romanelli, *Il comando impossibile. Stato e società nell'Italia liberale (Bologna, 1988)*.

3. P. Pombeni, *Partiti e sistemi politici nella storia contemporanea* (Bologna, 1994) 106–15.

4. F. Cammarano, 'La costrusione dello stato e la classe dirigente' *Storio d'Italia II: Il nuovo stato e la società civile*, eds, G. Sabbatucci and V. Vidotto (Bari–Rome, 1995), 3–112.

5. Quoted in O. Barie, ed. *Le origini dell'Italia contemporanea* (Bologna, 1966), 56.

6. C. Benso di Cavour, *Discorsi parlamentari*, 15 (Florence) speech of 21 April 1858.

7. 'Un deputato', 'Torniamo allo statuto', *Nuova Antologia*, 151 (1897), 24.

8. See A. Capone, *Destra e Sinistra da Cavour a Crispi* (Turin, 1981).

9. F. Crispi, *Carteggi politici inediti (1860–1900)*, ed., T Palamenghi-Crispi (Rome, undated), 457.

10. See F. Cammarano, *Il progresso moderato. Un'opposizione liberale nella svolta dell'Italia crispina (1887–1892)* (Bologna, 1990), 30–35; G. Carocci, *Agostino Depretis e la politica interna italiana dal 1876 al 1887* (Turin, 1956); ed., G. Carocci *Il trasformismo dall'Unità ad oggi* (Milan, 1992).

11. On these see ISAP. *Le riforme crispine*, 4 vols., (Milan, 1990).

12. See G Carocci, *Giolitti e l'età giolittiana* (Turin, 1961); G. Candeloro, *Storia dell'Italia moderna III. La crisi di fine secolo e l'età giolittiana.* (Milan, 1974); A. Aquarone, *L'Italia giolittiana*, (Bologna, 1988); E. Gentile, *Il mito dello stato nuovo dall'antigiolittismo al fascismo* (Bari–Rome, 1982).

13. See F. Gaeta, *Il nazionalismo italiano* (Bari, 1981).

14. Quoted in A. d'Orsi, ed., *I nazionalisti* (Milan, 1991).

Index